# EASY BOOTEES
# TO KNIT

# EASY BOOTEES TO KNIT

## Snuggly baby bootees for tiny toes

**PAVILION**

First published in the United Kingdom in 2014 by
Pavilion Books Company Limited
1 Gower Street
London
WC1E 6HD

ISBN 978-1-91023-116-6

A CIP catalogue record for this book is available
from the British Library.

10 9 8 7 6 5 4 3 2 1

Reproduction by Mission, Hong Kong
Printed and bound by 1010 Printing International Ltd, China

This book can be ordered direct from the publisher at
www.pavilionbooks.com

# Contents

# Knitting for babies

## Safety
Most babies are fascinated by their own feet at some point in their lives and will happily grab anything put onto them and try to pull it off. Therefore you should take note of the following safety tips when knitting bootees.

• When adding ribbons or ties to bootees you should attach them to the back of the bootee with a stitch. This will ensure that the baby can't pull them off.

• All buttons should be firmly stitched on with strong thread and checked periodically to ensure that they remain securely fastened so that the baby cannot pull them off.

• If you are embellishing bootees with stitched-on items, such as bells, pompoms or motifs, stitch them on firmly and check them as for buttons.

## Washing
Most bootees can be handwashed in gentle washing powder or as instructed on the yarn ball bands. Check washing instructions on any store-bought embellishments.

## Yarns

I have chosen a variety of yarns to make the bootees in this book. Most yarns these days are soft to touch, so they should not irritate a baby's delicate skin. However, if the baby suffers from eczema it is a good idea to choose to knit with cotton rather than wool or synthetic yarns.

## Seams

It is best to use a flat seam when sewing up bootees so that there is no ridge inside to rub against the skin. Lay the pieces out wrong-side up with the edges to be joined touching one another. Join the edges with oversewing stitches, matching the sides as you work. On roll-cuffed bootees you can reverse the seam on the top section of the cuff for a neat finish.

## Sizing small feet

When knitting bootees it is essential to check your tension (gauge) carefully (see page 12), as there is not much room for error in such tiny patterns. If you want to change the size of a pattern, try knitting it on larger or smaller needles. The foot sizes here are an approximate guide.

| | |
|---|---|
| 0–3 months | 9cm (3¾ in) |
| 3–6 months | 10cm (4in) |
| 6–9 months | 11.5cm (4½in) |

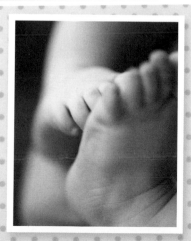

# Pattern information

## Abbreviations

The following abbreviations are those most commonly used in all the patterns. Where individual patterns have special abbreviations, these are explained at the beginning of the pattern. Where cast-off (bound-off) stitches are given in the middle of a row, the last stitch of the cast-off (bind-off) is always included in the instructions that follow.

**alt** = alternate

**beg** = beginning

**C** = contrast colour

**cont** = continue

**dec** = decrease by knitting the next 2 stitches together

**folls** = follows/following

**inc** = increase by knitting into the front and back of the next stitch

**k** = knit

**k2tog** = knit next 2 stitches together

**k3tog** = knit next 3 stitches together

**M** = main colour

**m1** = make stitch by picking up yarn before next stitch and knitting into the back of made loop

**moss stitch** (US: seed stitch):
(on even number of sts) Row 1: *k1, p1* to end; Row 2: *p1, k1* to end
(on odd number of sts) every row: *k1, p1* to last st, k1

**p** = purl

**p2tog** = purl next 2 stitches together

**p2togb** = purl next 2 stitches together through back of loops

**p3tog** = purl next 3 stitches together

**patt** = pattern

**psso** = pass slipped stitch over

**rem** = remain(ing)

**rep** = repeat

**RS** = right side

**s1** = slip next stitch

**st st** = stocking stitch (US: stockinette stitch)

**st(s)** = stitch(es)

**tog** = together

**WS** = wrong side

**yb** = yarn back

**yf** = yarn forward

**yo** = yarn around needle

**\*\*** = repeat enclosed instructions the number of times indicated

**[ ]** = brackets refer to larger size(s). Where only one figure is given it refers to all sizes

## Needle sizes

This table shows the conversions between metric and US needle sizes.

| Metric | US |
|--------|-----|
| 2.75mm | 12 |
| 3mm | 11 |
| 3.25mm | 10 |
| 3.75mm | 9 |
| 4mm | 8 |
| 4.5mm | 7 |
| 5mm | 6 |

## How to make a tension (gauge) square

Please check your own tension (what US knitters refer to as gauge) before you start. Some people find that they need to use a smaller needle when knitting cotton. Cast on at least 30 sts and work at least 40 rows. Measure only the stitches given (e.g. 22 sts by 28 rows) to check your tension. Remember that one stitch too many or too few over 10cm (4in) can spoil your work. If you have too many stitches, change to a larger needle; if you have too few, change to a smaller size. Then try again until the tension square is correct.

## Colour knitting

Most of the multicoloured designs
in this book are worked using the
Fair Isle technique where the yarn
is carried across the back of the
work. However, a few designs use
the intarsia method, which involves
using separate balls of contrast
colours, or shorter lengths wound
around bobbins, but NOT carrying
the main yarn across the back of
the section. Twist the yarns around
one another at the colour change to
avoid holes forming.

## Care instructions

Steam your knitting lightly by using
a warm iron over a damp cloth.
Never let the iron come directly
in contact with the knitting. Ease
the knitting into shape, or block it
out with pins until the steam has
completely dried off. For washing
instructions, see the yarn ball bands.

# Fair Isle and frill bootees

**Keep these pretty pastel bootees for special occasions. The frilled top is very effective, and very easy to knit.**

## Size
To fit baby of 6–9 months

## Materials
50g balls of 4ply (sport-weight)
   100% wool yarn: 1 x pink (M) and
   1 x cream (C)
Small amounts of mauve (A) and
   yellow yarn (B)
Pair of 3mm (US 2) needles
100cm (39in) of ribbon

## Tension (gauge)
28 sts and 38 rows = 10cm (4in) square
   over st st using 3mm (US 2) needles.

## Abbreviations
See pages 10–11.

## First bootee
### Cuff
Using C, cast on 122 sts and knit 1 row.
**Row 2:** P1, [*p3tog* three times, p2]
to end.
**Row 3:** Using M, *k2tog* twice, *k3,
k2tog* nine times, k3, *k2tog* twice.
(43 sts)
Work 8 rows in k1, p1 rib.
Change to st st, work 2 rows.
**Row 14:** *K3, yo, k2tog* four times, k1,
*to* four times k2.
Work 3 more rows.

### Divide for top of foot
K29, turn, p15, turn.
On 15 sts, work 22 rows.
Break yarn.
With RS facing (14 sts on needle), rejoin
M and pick up 15 sts along side of foot,
15 sts from toe, 15 sts along side of foot
and 14 sts on needle. (73 sts)
**Row 1:** Knit.
**Row 2:** Work Fair Isle following
instructions and chart: using C, knit.

**Row 3:** Purl *1B, 1C* to last st, 1B.
**Row 4:** Using C, knit.
**Row 5:** Purl, *1A, 3C* to last st, 1A.
**Row 6:** Knit *1B, 1A, 1C, 1A* to last st, 1B.
**Row 7:** As row 5.
**Row 8:** As row 4.
**Row 9:** Using B, dec, purl to last 2 sts, dec. Break yarns. (71 sts)

### Shape sole
Using M,
**Row 1:** K1, *k2tog, k29, k2tog* k3, *to* again, k1.
**Row 2:** K30, k2tog, k3, s1, k1, psso, k30.
**Row 3:** P1, *p2tog, k26, p2togb*, k3, *to* again, k1.
**Row 4:** K27, k2tog, k3, s1, k1, psso, k27.
**Row 5:** P1, *p2tog, k23, p2togb*, k3, *to* again, k1.
**Row 6:** K24, k2tog, k3, s1, k1, psso, k24
**Row 7:** Cast (bind) off.

## Second bootee
Make second bootee to match.

## Finishing
Join leg seam and under-foot seam. Weave in any loose ends. Cut ribbon in half, thread through eyelets and tie in bow (see page 8).

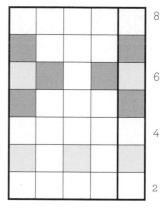

4 st rep

C ☐

B ☐

A ☐

# Cable bootees

These bootees feature a simple cable winding right around the baby's feet. The cable stands out when knitted in a contrast colour, but for a more subtle look you could knit the whole bootee in one colour.

## Size

To fit baby of 0–3[3–6:6–9] months

## Materials

50g balls of 4ply (sport-weight) wool
and cotton blend yarn: 1 x lilac (A)
and 1 x cream (B)
Pair of 3.25mm (US 3) needles
Cable needle

## Tension (gauge)

24 sts and 32 rows = 10cm (4in) square
over st st using 3.25mm (US 3)
needles.

## Abbreviations

**C6b** = slip 3 sts onto cable needle
and hold at back of work, k3 from
left-hand needle, then k3 from
cable needle.
See also pages 10–11.

## First bootee

### Cable strip

Using B, cast on 8 sts.
**Row 1:** Knit.
**Row 2:** K1, p6, k1.
**Rows 3–4:** As rows 1–2.
**Row 5:** K1, c6b, k1.
**Row 6:** As row 2.
**Rows 7–72[84:96]:** As rows 1–6, 11
[13:15] times, placing markers at each
end of row 37[43:49].
Work rows 1–2 again.
Cast (bind) off.

### Sole

Using A, pick up and knit 63[73:83]
sts along cable strip, 31[36:41] sts each
side of marked row and 1 st on marked
row.
**Rows 1–3:** Knit.
**Row 4:** K2, *s1, k1, psso, k25[30:35],
k2tog*, k1, *to* again, k2.
**Row 5:** Knit.
**Row 6:** K2, *s1, k1, psso, k23[28:33],
k2tog*, k1, *to* again, k2.
**Row 7:** Knit.
**Row 8:** K2, *s1, k1, psso, k21[26:31],
k2tog*, k1, *to* again, k2.
**Row 9:** Knit.
**Row 10:** Cast (bind) off.

## Upper

Using B, cast on 32[34:36] sts. Change
to A and knit 1 row. Work 15 rows in k1,
p1 rib.

Change to st st and work 4[6:8] rows.

**Rows 5–6:** Cast (bind) off 11 sts, work
to end.

On 10[12:14] sts, work 14[16:18] rows.
Cast (bind) off.

## Second bootee

Make second bootee to match.

## Finishing

Join sole and heel seam. Join leg
seam. Pin centre front of upper to
centre of cable strip. Ease upper shoe
to fit round cable strip and stitch into
position. Weave in any loose ends.

# Textured shoes

A great classic shape, these buttoned shoes are worked in cotton.
The simple design shows off the stitch texture well.

## Size
To fit baby of 3-6 months

## Materials
50g ball of 4ply (sport-weight) 100%
    cotton yarn: 1 x white
Pair of 2.75mm (US 2) needles
Safety pin (for stitch holder)
2 small buttons

## Tension (gauge)
28 sts and 38 rows = 10cm (4in) square
    over st st using 2.75mm (US 2)
    needles.

## Abbreviations
See pages 10–11.

## US terms
Moss stitch = seed stitch
    (see page 10).

## First shoe
### Sole
Cast on 24 sts and work in moss st.
Inc each end of rows 2, 4, 6 and 8.
(32 sts)
Work 3 rows. Dec each end of rows 12,
14, 16 and 18. (24 sts)
**Row 19:** Moss to end, cast on 8 sts.

### Upper
Inc beg of 2nd and every alt row to
38 sts. (Row 12)
**Row 13:** Cast (bind) off 12 sts, moss 3,
bind (cast) off 4 sts, moss to end.
**Row 14:** Moss 19, leave 3 sts on
safety pin.
**Rows 15–25:** Moss st.
**Row 26:** Moss 19, cast on 19 sts.
**Row 27:** Moss st.
**Row 28:** Dec, moss st to end.
**Rows 29–38:** As rows 27–28.
**Row 39:** Cast (bind) off.

## Strap

Place 3 sts from safety pin onto needle.

**Row 1:** Inc, inc, k1.

**Rows 2–15:** Moss st.

**Row 16:** Moss 2, cast (bind) off 1, moss 2.

**Row 17:** Moss 2, yo, moss 2.

**Rows 18–20:** Moss st.

**Row 21:** Cast (bind) off.

## Second shoe

Make second shoe to match.

## Finishing

Join heel seam. Carefully fit upper to sole, easing fullness around toe area, and stitch into position. Moss (seed) stitch is reversible so take care to stitch up the second shoe as a mirror image of the first shoe, so obtaining a left and a right shoe. Weave in any loose ends. Stitch on the buttons (see page 8).

# Anchor bootees

Neatly nautical, these bootees are great for all little sailors. Warm wool will keep tiny toes warm on the coldest days, at sea or on shore.

## Size
To fit baby of 3–6 months

## Materials
50g balls of 4ply (sport-weight) 100% wool yarn: 1 x navy (M) and 1 x cream (C)
Pair of 3mm (US 2) needles

## Tension (gauge)
28 sts and 38 rows = 10cm (4in) square over st st using 3mm (US 2) needles.

## Abbreviations
See pages 10–11.

## First bootee
### Cuff
Using C, cast on 42 sts. Change to M and work 6cm (2½in) in k1, p1 rib, dec end of last row. (41 sts)
Change to st st. Work 4 rows.

### Divide for top of foot
K28, turn, p15, turn.
On 15 sts, work 8 rows.
**Row 9:** Place anchor motif: knit 7M, 1C, 7M.
Work anchor motif then work 4 more rows (toe), break yarn.
With RS facing (13 sts on needle), rejoin M and pick up 11 sts along side of foot, 15 sts from toe, 11 sts along side of foot and 13 sts on needle. (63 sts)
Cont as follows:
**Row 1:** Using M, knit.
**Rows 2–3:** Using C, knit.
**Rows 4–5:** Using M, knit.
**Rows 6–13:** As rows 2–5 twice.
Break C.

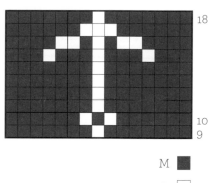

18

10
9

M ■

C □

## Shape sole
Using M,

**Row 1:** K1, *k2tog, k25, k2tog*, k3, *to* again, k1.

**Row 2:** K26, k2tog, k3, k2tog, k26.

**Row 3:** K1, *k2tog, k22, k2tog*, k3, *to* again, k1.

**Row 4:** K23, k2tog, k3, k2tog, k23.

**Row 5:** K1, *k2tog, k19, k2tog*, k3, *to* again, k1.

**Row 6:** Cast (bind) off.

## Second bootee
Make second bootee to match.

## Finishing
Join leg seam and under-foot seam (see page 9). Weave in any loose ends.

# Simple T-bar shoes

These are a popular design and the T-bar shape means that they can be buttoned onto the liveliest foot with confidence.

## Size
To fit baby of 6–9 months

## Materials
50g ball of 4ply (sport-weight) 100% mercerized cotton yarn: 1 x lilac
Pair of 3.25mm (US 3) needles
Safety pin (for stitch holder)
2 small buttons

## Tension (gauge)
24 sts and 30 rows = 10cm (4in) square over st st using 3.25mm (US 3) needles.

## Abbreviations
See pages 10–11.

## US terms
Moss stitch = seed stitch (see page 10).

## Right shoe
### Sole
Cast on 19 sts and work in moss st. Inc each end of rows 2, 4 and 6. (25 sts) Work 3 rows. Dec each end of rows 10, 12 and 14. (19 sts)
**Row 15:** Moss st to end, cast on 6 sts.

### Upper
**Row 1:** Knit.
**Row 2:** Inc, purl to end.
**Rows 3–6:** As rows 1–2 twice.
**Row 7:** Knit.
**Row 8:** Inc, p10, moss 17.
**Row 9:** Moss 17, k12.
**Row 10:** Inc, p11, moss 17. (30 sts)
**Row 11:** Cast (bind) off 10 sts, moss 3, cast (bind) off 2 sts, moss 2, k13.
**Row 12:** P13, moss 2, leave 3 sts on safety pin.
**Row 13:** Moss 2, k13.
**Rows 14–21:** As rows 12–13 four times, placing markers on rows 16, 17 and 18 at moss-st end.
**Row 22:** P13, moss 2, cast on 15 sts.

**Row 23:** Moss 17, k13.
**Row 24:** P2tog, p11, moss 17.
**Row 25:** Moss 17, k12.
**Row 26:** P2tog, purl to end.
**Rows 27–32:** Work in st st, dec beg of each purl row. (25 sts)
**Row 33:** Cast (bind) off.

### Strap A
Place 3 sts from safety pin onto needle.
**Rows 1–15:** Moss st.
**Row 16:** Moss 1, bind (cast) off 1, moss 1.
**Row 17:** Moss 1, yo, moss 1.
**Rows 18–19:** Moss st.
**Row 20:** Cast (bind) off.

### Strap B
RS facing, pick up 3 sts from marker on rows 16, 17 and 18. Work 20 rows in moss st. Cast (bind) off.

## Left shoe
### Sole
As for right shoe.

### Upper
Rev st st, eg:
**Row 1:** Purl.
**Row 2:** Inc, knit to end.
**Row 8:** Inc, k10, moss 17.

## Finishing
Join heel seam. Carefully fit upper to sole, easing fullness around toe area, and stitch into position. Weave in any loose ends. Fold centre strap B over to make a loop for cross strap A. Stitch in place. Thread strap A through loop. Stitch on buttons (see page 8).

# Polka-dot socks

Fun and functional, these socks look great in almost any colour combination, so they are perfect for using up small quantities of yarns.

## Size
To fit baby of 3–6 months

## Materials
50g balls of 4ply (sport-weight)
    100% wool yarn: 1 x blue (M) and
    1 x cream (C)
4 double-pointed 3mm (US 2) needles

## Tension (gauge)
28 sts and 38 rows = 10cm (4in) square
    over st st using 3mm (US 2) needles.

## Abbreviations
See pages 10–11.

## First sock
Note: place marker at beginning
of round.

## Cuff
Using M, cast on 32 sts (10, 10 and 12 sts). Work 3 rounds in *k1, p1* to end. Change to every round, knit.

**Round 4:** M.
**Round 5:** 2C, 6M.
**Rounds 6–7:** 3C, 4M, 1C.
**Round 8:** As round 5.
**Round 9:** M.
**Round 10:** 4M, 2C, 2M.
**Rounds 11–12:** 3M, 4C, 1M.
**Round 13:** As round 10.
**Rounds 14–18:** As rounds 4 8.

## Start heel
**Round 19:** Using M, k15 and turn, leave rem sts on needles for instep. On 15 sts, work 7 rows in st st, starting with a purl row.

## Shape heel
**Row 1:** K9, turn.
**Row 2:** S1, p2, turn.
**Row 3:** S1, k1, s1, k1, psso, k1, turn.
**Row 4:** S1, p2, p2tog, p1, turn.
**Row 5:** S1, k3, s1, k1, psso, k1, turn.
**Row 6:** S1, p4, p2tog, p1, turn.
**Row 7:** S1, k5, s1, k1, psso, turn.
**Row 8:** S1, p6, p2tog, p1.
Break yarn.

Using M, pick up and knit 6 sts along heel, 9 sts from needle, 6 sts along heel, k16 from instep sts, move round marker to here and last st to left-hand needle.

Cont as folls:
**Round 1:** S1, k1, psso, 5M, 2C, 6M, 2C, 3M, 2togM, 5M, 2C, 6M, 2C, 1M.
**Round 2:** S1, k1, psso, 3M, 4C, 4M, 4C, 1M, 2togM, *4M, 4C* twice.
**Round 3:** S1, k1, psso, 2M, 4C, 4M, 4C, 2togM, *4M, 4C* twice.
**Round 4:** *4M, 2C, 2M* to end.
Cont in patt to completion of round 24.
Break C.

## Shape toe
Using M,
**Round 1:** Knit.
**Round 2:** *K2tog, k11, s1, k1, psso* twice.
**Round 3:** Knit.
**Round 4:** *K2tog, k9, s1, k1, psso* twice.
**Round 5:** Knit.
**Round 6:** *K2tog, k7, s1, k1, psso* twice.
**Round 7:** Knit.
**Round 8:** Cast (bind) off.

# Second sock
Make second sock to match.

# Finishing
Join toe seam (see page 9). Weave in any loose ends.

# Daisy lace bootees

The lace flower on the toes is pretty, but not too fussy, making these a great everyday bootee.

## Size
To fit baby of 0–3 months

## Materials
50g balls of 4ply (sport-weight)
   100% wool yarn: 1 x cream (M)
   and 1 x pink (C)
Pair of 3mm (US 2) needles
100cm (39in) of ribbon

## Tension (gauge)
28 sts and 38 rows = 10cm (4in) square
   over st st using 3mm (US 2) needles.

## Abbreviations
See pages 10–11.

## First bootee
### Cuff
Using C, cast on 41 sts and work
10 rows in st st.
Change to M and work 6 rows.
**Row 7:** K2, *yo, k2tog, k2* nine times,
yo, k2tog, k1.
Work 3 more rows.

### Divide for top of foot
K28, turn, p15 turn.
On 15 sts, work 6 rows.
**Row 7:** K7, yo, s1, k1, psso, k6.
**Row 8 and alt rows:** Purl.
**Row 9:** K4, k2tog, yo, k3, yo, s1, k1, psso, k4.

**Row 11:** K3, k2tog, yo, k2, yo, s1, k1,
psso, k1, yo, s1, k1, psso, k3.
**Row 13:** As row 9.
**Row 15:** As row 7.
Work 7 more rows. Break yarn.
With RS facing (13 sts on needle),
rejoin M and pick up 11 sts along side
of foot, 15 sts from toe, 11 sts along side
of foot and 13 sts on needle. (63 sts)
Knit 13 rows.

### Shape sole
**Row 1:** K1, *k2tog, k25, k2tog*, k3, *to*
again, k1.
**Row 2:** K26, k2tog, k3, k2tog, k26.
**Row 3:** K1, *k2tog, k22, k2tog*, k3, *to*
again, k1.
**Row 4:** K23, k2tog, k3, k2tog, k23.
**Row 5:** K1, *k2tog, k19, k2tog*, k3, *to*
again, k1.
**Row 6:** Cast (bind) off.

## Second bootee
Make second bootee to match.

## Finishing
Join leg seam and under-foot seam.
Weave in any loose ends. Cut ribbon
in half, thread through eyelets and tie
in bow (see page 8).

# Pixie boots

Perfect for your own little pixie, these lace-up boots are smart and original.
You could knit them in a pale colour and lace them with ribbons to make a
little girl's feet especially pretty.

## Size
To fit baby of 3-6 months

## Materials
50g ball of DK (light worsted)
  100% merino wool yarn: 1 x green
Small amount of red yarn
Pair of 3.25mm (US 3) needles
Safety pin (for stitch holder)

## Tension (gauge)
24 sts and 32 rows = 10cm (4in)
  square over st st using 3.25mm
  (US 3) needles.

## Abbreviations
See pages 10–11.

## US terms
Moss stitch = seed stitch
  (see page 10).

## First boot
### Sole
Start at toe end. Cast on 2 sts. Work in
moss st. Inc each end rows 1, 3 and 5.
Cont until work measures 7cm (2¾in).
Dec each end of next and alt rows to
2 sts, k2tog, fasten off.

## Upper

Start at toe end. Cast on 2 sts.

**Row 1:** Inc in both sts.
**Row 2:** K1, inc, inc, k1.
**Row 3:** Purl.
**Row 4:** K1, inc in next 4 sts, k1.
**Row 5:** Purl.
**Row 6:** K3, inc in next 4 sts, k3.
**Row 7:** Purl.
**Row 8:** K5, inc in next 4 sts, k5. (18 sts)
**Row 9:** P4, moss 10, p4.
**Row 10:** K4, moss 10, k4.
**Row 11:** As row 9.
**Row 12:** K4, moss 3, cast (bind) off 4 sts, moss 3, k4.
**Row 13:** P4, moss 3.
**Row 14:** Moss 3, k4.
**Row 15:** P4, k1, yo, k2tog.
**Row 16:** As row 14.
**Rows 17–22:** As rows 13-14 three times.
**Rows 23–24:** As rows 15-16.
**Row 25:** P4, place 3 sts on safety pin. Work 10 rows in st st.
Cast (bind) off.
Rejoin yarn to rem sts and work to match.
Join heel seam.

## Cuff

With RS facing, moss 3 from safety pin, pick up and knit 9 sts to heel, 1 st from seam, 9 sts from heel to safety pin, moss 3.

**Rows 1–4:** Moss 3, rib 19, moss 3.
**Row 5:** K2tog, yo, moss 1, rib 19, moss 1, yo, k2tog.
**Rows 6–10:** As row 1 five times.
**Row 11:** As row 5.
**Rows 12–13:** Cast (bind) off 3, work to end.
**Row 14:** Moss 3, purl to last 3 sts, moss 3.
**Row 15:** Moss 3, m1, knit to last 3 sts, m1, moss 3.
**Row 16:** As row 14.
**Row 17:** Moss 3, knit to last 3 sts, moss 3.
**Row 18:** Moss 3, m1, purl to last 3 sts, m1, moss 3.
**Rows 19–20:** As rows 15-16.
**Rows 21–23:** Moss st.
**Row 24:** Cast (bind) off.

## Second boot

Make second boot to match.

## Finishing

Weave in any loose ends. Plait three lengths of red yarn together to make laces, knotting ends to secure them. Thread laces through eyelets (see photograph and page 8).

# Gingham shoes

A design for more experienced Fair Isle knitters, these shoes are so pretty and sweet that, tied with a sheer ribbon, they are perfect for little princesses.

## Size
To fit baby of 6–9 months

## Materials
50g balls of 4ply (sport-weight) 100% mercerized cotton yarn: 1 x pink (M) and 1 x white (C)
Pair 2.75mm (US 2) needles
40cm (16in) of ribbon

## Tension (gauge)
26 sts and 34 rows = 10cm (4in) square over Fair Isle using 2.75mm (US 2) needles.

## Abbreviations
See pages 10–11.

## US terms
Moss stitch = seed stitch (see page 10).

## First shoe
### Sole
Using M, cast on 24 sts and work in moss st.
Inc each end of rows 2, 4, 6 and 8. (32 sts)
Work 3 rows. Dec each end of rows 12, 14, 16 and 18. (24 sts)

**Row 19:** Moss to end, cast on 8 sts. (32 sts)

**Upper**

Change to st st.

**Row 1:** *3M, 3C* to last 2 sts, 2M.

**Row 2:** Inc, 1M, *3C, 3M* to end. (33 sts)

**Row 3:** *3M, 3C* to last 3 sts, 3M.

**Row 4:** Inc, 2M, *3C, 3M* to end. (34 sts)

**Row 5:** *3C, 3M* to last 4 sts, 3C, 1M.

**Row 6:** Inc, *3C, 3M* to last 3 sts, 3C. (35 sts)

**Row 7:** *3C, 3M* to last 5 sts, 3C, 2M.

**Row 8:** Inc, 1M, *3C, 3M* to last 3 sts, 3C. (36 sts)

**Row 9:** *3M, 3C* to end.

**Row 10:** Inc, 2C, *3M, 3C* twice, 21M. (37 sts)

**Row 11:** Using M, *k1, p1* six times, yo, p2tog, *k1, p1* three times, k1, knit *3C, 3M* twice, 3C, 1M. (37 sts)

**Row 12:** Inc, purl *3C, 3M* twice, 3C, using M, *k1, p1* to last st, k1. (38 sts)

**Row 13:** Using M, cast (bind) off 18 sts, p1, k1, knit *3M, 3C* twice, 3M, 2C. (20 sts)

**Row 14:** Purl 2C, *3M, 3C* twice, using M, p3, k1, p1, k1.

**Row 15:** Using M, k1, p1, k4, knit *3C, 3M* twice, 2C.

**Rows 16–24:** Keep gingham patt correct (3 sts/4 rows), with 3-st moss edging in M.

**Row 25:** Cast on 18 sts, using M, *k1, p1* six times, yo, p2tog, *k1, p1* three times, k1, knit *3C, 3M* twice, 3C, 2M. (38 sts)

**Row 26:** P2togM, *3C, 3M* twice, 3C, moss 21 sts. (37 sts)

**Row 27:** Using M, moss 21, knit *3C, 3M* twice, 3C, 1M.

**Row 28:** P2togC, purl 2C, *3M, 3c* to end.

**Rows 29–36:** Work 8 rows in gingham patt, dec beg of each purl row.

**Row 37:** Cast (bind) off.

With RS facing and using M, pick up 21 sts from heel to front, 12 sts across gingham and 21 sts from front to heel. Work as folls:

**Row 1:** Moss 12, dec, yo, moss 6, dec, moss 10, dec, moss 6, yo, dec, moss 12.

**Row 2:** Moss st.

**Row 3:** Cast (bind) off.

## Second shoe

Make second shoe to match, reversing the shaping.

## Finishing

Join heel seam. Fit upper to sole, easing fullness around toe, and stitch into position. Weave in loose ends. Cut ribbon in half, thread through eyelets and tie in bow (see page 8).

# Lace and heart bootees

A combination of lacy cuffs and an intarsia motif make these charming bootees a good design for more experienced knitters to try their hand at. Ribbon ties will help to keep the bootees securely on a baby's feet.

## Size
To fit baby of 3–6[6–9] months

## Materials
50g balls of 4ply (sport-weight)
  100% wool yarn: 1 x cream (M)
Small amount of red yarn (C)
Pair each of 3.25mm (US 3) and 3mm
  (US 2) needles
100cm (39in) of ribbon

## Tension (gauge)
28 sts and 38 rows = 10cm (4in)
  square over st st using 3.25mm
  (US 3) needles.

## Abbreviations
See pages 10–11.

## First bootee
### Cuff
Using C and 3.25mm (US 3) needles, cast on 51 sts.
Change to M.
**Row 1:** Knit.
**Row 2:** K2, yo, k2, s1, k2tog, psso, k2, *yo, k1, yo, k2, s1, k2tog, psso, k2* five times, yo, k2.
**Rows 3–18:** As rows 1–2 eight times.
**Row 19:** Knit.
**Row 20:** Change to 3mm (US 2) needles, p2, *p2tog, p3* nine times, p2tog, p2. (41 sts)
Change to st st. Work 2 rows.
**Row 3:** K2, *yo, k2tog, k2* nine times, yo, k2tog, k1.
Work 3 more rows.

### Divide for top of foot
K28, turn, p15, turn.
On 15 sts, work 6[8] rows.

**Row 7[9]:** Place heart motif following instructions and chart: knit 5M, 2C, 1M, 2C, 5M,
Work heart motif then work 2[4] more rows (toe), break yarn.
With RS facing (13 sts on needle), rejoin M and pick up 11[16]sts along side of foot, 15 sts from toe, 11[16]sts along side of foot and 13 sts on needle. (63:73 sts)
Knit 13 rows.

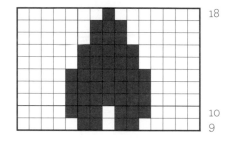

M ☐

C ■

### Shape sole

**Row 1:** K1, *k2tog, k25[30], k2tog* k3, *to* again, k1.
**Row 2:** K26[31], k2tog, k3, k2tog, k26[31].
**Row 3:** K1, *k2tog, k22[27], k2tog* k3, *to* again, k1.
**Row 4:** K23[28], k2tog, k3, k2tog, k23[28].
**Row 5:** K1, *k2tog, k19[24], k2tog* k3, *to* again, k1.
**Row 6:** Cast (bind) off.

### Second bootee

Make second bootee to match.

### Finishing

Join leg seam and under-foot seam. Weave in any loose ends. Cut ribbon in half, thread through eyelets and tie in bow (see page 8).

# Pirate boots

This stripy design is perfect for bold little boys. As the boots are knitted in wool, they will keep little feet warm on the windiest days out.

## Size
To fit baby of 3–6 months

## Materials
50g balls of DK (light worsted)
100% wool yarn: 1 x blue (A), 1 x cream (B) and 1 x red (C)
Pair of 2.75mm (US 2) needles

## Tension (gauge)
24 sts and 32 rows = 10cm (4in) square over st st using 2.75mm (US 2) needles.

## Abbreviations
See pages 10–11.

## First boot
### Sole
Start at heel end. Using C, cast on 3 sts and work in seed (moss) st. Inc each end of rows 2, 3, 5, 6 and 8. (13 sts). Cont without shaping to completion of row 36. Dec each end of next and every alt row to 5 sts.
**Next row:** Purl.
Change to st st and work in stripes of 4 rows B, 4 rows A. Shaping rows only given.

### Upper
**Row 1:** Inc in 4 sts, k1. (9 sts)
**Row 3:** K1, inc in 2 sts, k2, inc in 2 sts, k2. (13 sts)
**Row 5:** K2, inc in 2 sts, k4, inc in 2 sts, k3. (17 sts)
**Row 7:** K3, inc, k8, inc, k4. (19 sts)
**Row 10:** *P2, inc* twice, p6, *inc, p2* twice, p1. (23 sts)
**Row 25:** K10, cast (bind) off 3 sts, k10. On 10 sts,
**Row 27:** K1, k2tog, knit to end.

**Row 29:** As row 27.
**Row 31:** As row 27. (7 sts)
Work to completion of row 46.
Cast (bind) off.
Rejoin yarn to rem sts at centre front.
**Row 26:** WS facing, purl.
**Row 27:** Knit to last 3sts, s1, k1,
psso, k1.
Cont decs as set and work to match
first side.

### Cuff
With RS facing and using C, pick up
and knit 35 sts around ankle. Work 11
rows in k1, p1 rib. Cast (bind) off.

## Second boot
Make second boot to match.

## Finishing
Join cuff and heel seam, pin to heel
end of sole. Carefully pin upper to sole,
easing any excess around toe area,
and stitch into position. Weave in any
loose ends.

# Sheep bootees

Soft and fluffy, these bootees will look lovely on your own little lamb. Ribbons in the cuffs will help to keep them in place.

## Size
To fit baby aged 3–6 months

## Materials
50g ball of DK (light worsted)
  100% wool yarn: 1 x black (A)
50g ball of aran (worsted) weight
  100% wool yarn: 1 x cream (B)
Pair each of 3.25mm (US 3) and 4.5mm
  (US 7) needles
76cm (30in) of ribbon

## Tension (gauge)
16 sts and 26 rows = 10cm (4in) square
  over st st using aran-weight yarn and
  4.5mm (US 7) needles.

## Abbreviations
See pages 10–11.

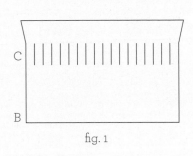

fig. 1

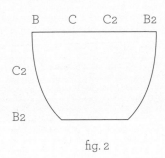

fig. 2

## First bootee
### Sole
Using 3.25mm (US 3) needles and A, cast on 3 sts. Work in garter st.
Inc each end of first and every alt row to 9 sts.
Cont without shaping until work measures 9cm ($3^1/_2$in).
Dec each end of next and every alt row to 3sts.
Cast (bind) off.

### Back and heel
Using 4.5mm (US 7) needles and B, cast on 18 sts and work 6 rows in st st.
**Rows 7–10:** Work in k1, p1 rib.
Work 10 more rows in st st, inc each end of rows 1, 3 and 5. Cast (bind) off.

### Front and toe
Using 4.5mm (US 7) needles and B, cast on 8 sts.
**Row 1:** K2, inc in next 3 sts, k3.
**Row 2:** Purl.
**Row 3:** K2, inc in next 6 sts, k3. (17 sts)
**Row 4:** Purl.
Work 15 rows more in st st.
**Row 20:** Cast (bind) off knitwise.
Mark 7th and 10th sts (C1 and C2 in fig. 2 on opposite page).

### Ears (make 2)
Using 3.25mm (US 3) needles and A, cast on 8 sts and work 5 rows in st st.
Dec each end of next 2 rows.
Work 1 row.
Inc each end of next 2 rows.
Work 4 more rows. Cast (bind) off.

## Second bootee
Make second bootee to match.

## Finishing
Front and toe – purl side is right side. Fold front in half lengthwise and join cast-on edge, A to A, to make toe (see fig. 2 opposite).

Back and heel – knit side is right side. Join back and heel section to front by stitching seams B1–C1 and B2–C2 (see figs. 1 and 2 opposite).

Join upper to sole. Weave in any loose ends.

Fold ears in half and stitch side seams, then stitch to bootees. Embroider nose and eyes using black yarn (see photograph). Turn over cuff at ankle and stitch down. Cut ribbon in half and thread through cuff (see page 8).

# Herringbone bootees

With their understated textured cuffs and scalloped trim, these bootees are ideal for special occasions as well as everyday wear.

## Size
To fit baby of 0–3[3–6] months

## Materials
50g ball of 4ply (sport-weight)
   100% cotton yarn: 1 x pale blue (M)
Small amount of white yarn (C)
Pair of 3mm (US 2) needles

## Tension (gauge)
28 sts and 38 rows = 10cm (4in) square
   over st st using 3mm (US 2) needles.

## Abbreviations
**M1** = place yarn before next stitch onto
   left-hand needle and knit it.
See also pages 10–11.

## First bootee
### Cuff
Using C, cast on 51 sts. Change to M
and work as folls:
**Row 1 (WS):** Purl.
**Row 2:** K1, k2tog, *k2, m1, k1, m1, k2,
s1, k2tog, psso* five times, k2, m1, k1,
m1, k2, s1, k1, psso, k1.
Rep rows 1 and 2 until work measures
4cm (1½in), ending with row 2.
**Next row:** *P2, p2tog, p1* to last st, p1.
(41 sts)
Work 3cm (1¼in) in k1, p1 rib, ending
with a RS row.
WS facing, change to st st (first row,
knit) and work 4 rows.

## Divide for top of foot
K28 turn, p15 turn.
On 15 sts, work 16[22] rows.
Break yarn.
With RS facing (13 sts on needle),
rejoin M and pick up 11[17] sts along
side of foot, 15 sts from toe, 11[17] sts
along side of foot and 13 sts on needle.
(63:75 sts)
Knit 13 rows.

## Shape sole
**Row 1:** K1, *k2tog, k25[31], k2tog*, k3,
*to* again, k1.
**Row 2:** K26[32], k2tog, k3, k2tog,

k26[32].

**Row 3:** K1, *k2tog, k22[28], k2tog*, k3, *to* again, k1.

**Row 4:** K23[29], k2tog, k3, k2tog, k23[29].

**Row 5:** K1, *k2tog, k19[25], k2tog*, k3, *to* again, k1.

**Row 6:** Cast (bind) off.

## Second bootee

Make second bootee to match.

## Finishing

Join leg seam and under-foot seam (see page 9). Weave in any loose ends.

# Fleur de lys socks

**This is a traditional and slightly more complicated design that is perfect for more experienced knitters who enjoy working Fair Isle patterns.**

## Size
To fit baby of 3–6 months

## Materials
50g ball of 4ply (sport-weight)
  100% merino wool yarn:
  1 x cream (M)
Small amounts of red (A) and blue (B)
4 double-pointed 3mm (US 2) needles

## Tension (gauge)
28 sts and 38 rows = 10cm (4in) square
  over st st using 3mm (US 2) needles.

## Abbreviations
See pages 10–11.

## First sock
Note: place marker at beginning
of round.

## Cuff
Using B, cast on 32 sts (10, 10 and
12 sts). Work 5 rounds in *k1, p1*
to end.
**Round 6:** Knit *3M, 1A* to end.
**Round 7:** *1A, 1M, 2A* to end.
**Round 8:** As round 6.
**Round 9:** *1M, 1B, 2M* to end.
**Round 10:** *3B, 1M* to end.
**Round 11:** As round 9.
**Rounds 12–17:** As rounds 6–11.
**Rounds 18–20:** As rounds 6–8.

## Start heel
**Round 21:** using B, k15, turn, leave
rem sts on needles for instep.
On 15 sts, work 7 rows in st st, starting
with a purl row.

## Shape heel

**Row 1:** K9, turn.
**Row 2:** S1, p2 turn.
**Row 3:** S1, k1, s1, k1, psso, k1, turn.
**Row 4:** S1, p2, p2tog, p1, turn.
**Row 5:** S1, k3, s1, k1, psso, k1, turn.
**Row 6:** S1, p4, p2tog, p1, turn.
**Row 7:** S1, k5, s1, k1, psso, turn.
**Row 8:** S1, p6, p2tog, p1.
Break yarn.
Using B, pick up and knit 6 sts from side heel, knit 9 sts from needle, pick up and knit 6 sts from side of heel. Break yarn.

**Right side facing:** Return to round marker. Take last st of last round and move it to left-hand needle to be first st of round.
Cont as folls:
**Round 1:** S1, 1B, psso, *3M, 1B* four times, 3M, 2togB, 1M, *1B, 3M* three times, 1B, 1M.
**Round 2:** S1, 1B, psso, *1M, 3B* four times, 1M, 2togM, *3B, 1M* three times, 3B.
**Round 3:** S1, 1M, psso, 1M, *1B, 3M* three times, 1B, 1M, 2togM, 1M, *1B, 3M* three times, 1B, 1M.
**Rounds 4–24:** Cont in patt. Break M and A.

## Shape toe

Using B,
**Round 1:** Knit.
**Round 2:** *K2tog, k12, s1, k1, psso* twice.
**Round 3:** Knit.
**Round 4:** *K2tog, k10, s1, k1, psso* twice.
**Round 5:** Knit.
**Round 6:** *K2tog, k8, s1, k1, psso* twice.
**Round 7:** Knit.
**Round 8:** Cast (bind) off.

## Second sock

Make second sock to match.

## Finishing

Join toe seam (see page 9). Weave in any loose ends.

# Knot shoes

These lovely, fluffy shoes simply tie round a baby's foot for a perfect fit. They look very modern and stylish, too.

## Size
To fit baby of 0–3 months

## Materials
25g ball of lace-weight silk and kid
    mohair blend: 1 x orange
Pair of 2.75mm (US 2) needles

## Tension (gauge)
28 sts and 28 rows = 10cm (4in) square
    over garter st using 2.75mm (US 2)
    needles.

## Abbreviations
See pages 10–11.

## First shoe
Note: use two ends of yarn throughout.

### Sole
Cast on 24 sts and work in garter st.
Inc each end of rows 2, 4, 6 and 8.
(32 sts)
Work 3 rows. Dec each end of rows 12,
14, 16 and 18. (24 sts)
**Row 19:** Knit to end, cast on 8 sts.

### Upper
**Row 1:** Knit.
**Row 2:** Inc, knit to end.
**Rows 3–12:** As rows 1–2 five times.
(38 sts)
**Row 13:** Cast (bind) off 19 sts, knit
to end.
**Rows 14–25:** Knit.
**Row 26:** Knit to end, cast on 19 sts.
**Row 27:** Knit.
**Row 28:** K2tog, knit to end.
**Rows 29–38:** As 27–28 five times.
**Row 39:** Cast (bind) off.

## Ties (make 2)

Cast on 40 sts.

**Row 1:** Knit.

**Row 2:** Cast (bind) off 2 sts, knit to end.

**Row 3:** Knit to last 2 sts, k2tog.

**Rows 4–5:** As rows 2–3.

**Row 6:** Cast (bind) off.

## Second shoe

Make second shoe to match.

### Finishing

Join heel seam. Carefully fit upper to sole, easing fullness around toe area, and stitch into position. Weave in any loose ends. Sew the square end of tie to each side of shoe, about 1cm (½in) from front (see photograph and page 8).

# Zebra bootees

Fashionable and funky for trendy toes, these bootees are practical, too, as the deep cuffs will help to keep them firmly on wriggling feet and kicking legs.

## Size
To fit baby of 3–6 months

## Materials
50g balls of 4ply (sport-weight)
   100% mercerized cotton yarn:
   1 x black (A) and 1 x cream (B)
Pair of 2.75mm (US 2) needles

## Tension (gauge)
26 sts and 34 rows = 10cm (4in) square
   over st st using 2.75mm (US 2) needles.

## Abbreviations
See pages 10–11.

## First bootee
### Sole
Start at heel end. Using A, cast on 3 sts and work in seed (moss) st. Inc each end of rows 2, 3, 5, 6 and 8. (13 sts)
Cont without shaping to completion of row 36.
Dec each end of next and every alt row to 5 sts.

**Next row:** Purl.

### Upper
Cont in st st.
**Row 1:** Inc A, inc B, 1A, inc B, inc A. (9 sts)
**Row 2:** 2A, 2B, 1A, 2B, 2A.
**Row 3:** 1A, inc A, inc B, 1B, 1A, 1B, inc B, inc A, 1A. (13 sts)
**Row 4:** 3A, 2B, 2A, 3B, 3A.
**Row 5:** 2A, inc A, inc B, 1B, 3A, 1B, inc B, inc A, 2A. (17 sts)
**Row 6:** 3A, 3B, 2A, 1B, 2A, 3B, 3A.
**Row 7:** 3A, inc B, *1B, 1A* twice, inc B, 1B, 3A. (19 sts)
**Row 8:** 2A, 3B, 4A, 2B, 3A, 3B, 2A.
**Row 9:** 1A, 3B, 4A, 2B, 4A, 3B, 2A.
**Row 10:** 2A, inc A, 2B, inc A, 1B, 2A, 2B, 1A, 1B, inc A, 2A, inc B, 2B. (23 sts)
**Rows 11–44:** Work zebra patt following chart.
**Row 45:** Cast (bind) off.
Rejoin yarn to rem sts of centre front.
**Row 26:** WS facing, 1B, 3A, 1B, 2A.

**Row 27:** 1B, 3A, 1B, 2A, s1, 1B, psso, 1B. Cont decs as set and work to match first side.

## Cuff

With RS facing and using A, pick up 35 sts around ankle.
Work 26 rows in k1, p1 rib.
Ws facing, change to B and knit 1 row.
Cast (bind) off.

## Second bootee

Make second bootee to match.

## Finishing

Join cuff seam, pin to heel end of sole. Carefully pin upper to sole, easing any excess around toe area, and stitch into position. Weave in loose ends.

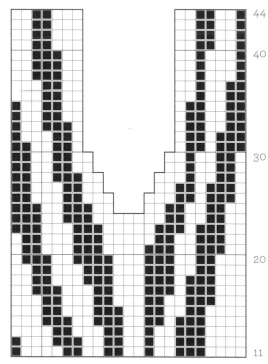

■ A
☐ B

# Heart T-bar shoes

The classic T-bar shoe is given extra appeal with a simple heart motif.
Try knitting the shoes in a pastel colour with a pale heart as well.

## Size
To fit baby of 3–6 months

## Materials
50g balls of 4ply (sport-weight)
    100% mercerized cotton yarn:
    1 x dark blue (M)
Small amount of red yarn (C)
Pair of 3.25mm (US 3) needles
2 small buttons

## Tension (gauge)
26 sts and 30 rows = 10cm (4in)
    square over Fair Isle using 3.25mm
    (US 3) needles.

## Abbreviations
See pages 10–11.

## US terms
Moss stitch = seed stitch
(see page 10).

## First shoe
### Sole
Using M, cast on 19 sts and work in
moss st.
Inc each end of rows 2, 4 and 6.
(25 sts)
Work 2 rows. Dec each end of rows 9,
11 and 13. (19 sts)
**Row 14:** Cast (bind) off.

### Upper
Using M, cast on 59 sts. Work as folls:
**Rows 1–9:** *K1, p1* to last st, k1.
**Row 10:** RS facing, moss 24, k10, s1, k1,
psso, turn.
**Row 11:** S1, p9, p2tog, turn.
**Row 12:** Place heart motif following
instructions and chart: s1, knit 4M, 1C,
4M, s1, k1, psso, turn.
**Row 13:** S1, purl 3M, 3C, 3M, p2tog,
turn.
**Row 14:** S1, knit 2M, 5C, 2M, s1, k1,
psso, turn.
**Row 15:** S1, purl 2M, 5C, 2M, p2tog,
turn.

**Row 16:** S1, knit 1M, 7C, 1M, s1, k1, psso, turn.

**Row 17:** S1, purl 1M, 7C, 1M, p2tog, turn.

**Row 18:** S1, knit 2M, 2C, 1M, 2C, 2M, s1, k1, psso, turn. Break C.

**Row 19:** As row 11.

**Row 20:** S1, k9, s1, k1, psso, turn.

**Row 21:** As row 11. (47 sts)

**Row 22:** S1, *p1, k1* to end.

**Row 23:** Moss across all sts, marking sts 8 and 39.

**Row 24:** Cast (bind) off 22 sts, moss 3 sts, cast (bind) off 22 sts.

### Strap A

Rejoin yarn to 3 sts and work 6cm (2½in) in moss st.
Cast (bind) off.

### Second shoe

Make second shoe to match.

### Finishing

Weave in any loose ends.

### Right strap B

Join heel seam. Cast on 3 sts, with RS facing pick up and knit 17 sts around heel between marked sts, cast on 15 sts, work as folls:

**Row 1:** *K1, p1* to last st, k1.

**Row 2:** *K1, p1* to last 4 sts, p2tog, yo, p1, k1.

**Row 3:** As row 1.

**Row 4:** Cast (bind) off.

### Left strap B

Cast on 15 sts, with RS facing, pick up and knit 17 sts around heel between marked sts, cast on 3 sts, work as folls:

**Row 1:** *K1, p1* to last st, k1.

**Row 2:** K1, p1, yo, p2tog, *k1, p1* to last st, k1.

**Row 3:** As row 1.

**Row 4:** Cast (bind) off.

Carefully pin sole to upper and stitch into position. Weave in any loose ends. Fold centre strap (A) over to make loop for cross strap. Stitch in place. Thread strap (B) through loop. Sew on buttons (see page 8).

# Bee shoes

These fun little shoes are bold and simple and are bound to get you, and your baby, noticed.

## Size
To fit baby of 3–6 months

## Materials
50g balls of 4ply (sport-weight)
    100% mercerized cotton yarn:
    1 x black (A) and 1 x yellow (B)
Pair of 2.75mm (US 2) needles

## Tension (gauge)
26 sts and 34 rows = 10cm (4in)
    square over st st using 2.75mm
    (US 2) needles.

## Abbreviations
See pages 10–11.

## First shoe
### Sole
Start at heel end. Using A, cast on 3 sts and work in moss (seed) st. Inc each end of rows 2, 3, 5, 6 and 8. (13 sts) Cont without shaping to completion of row 36. Dec each end of next and every alt row to 5 sts.
**Next row:** Purl.
Change to st st and work in stripes of 4 rows B, 4 rows A. Shaping rows only given.

### Upper
**Row 1:** Inc in 4 sts, k1. (9 sts)
**Row 3:** K1, inc in 2 sts, k2, inc in 2 sts, k2. (13 sts)
**Row 5:** K2, inc in 2 sts, k4, inc in 2 sts, k3. (17 sts)
**Row 7:** K3, inc, k8, inc, k4. (19 sts)
**Row 10:** *P2, inc* twice, p6, *inc, p2* twice, p1. (23 sts)
**Row 25:** K10, cast (bind) off 3 sts, k10. On 10 sts:
**Row 27:** K1, k2tog, knit to end.

**Row 29:** As row 27.
**Row 31:** As row 27. (7 sts)
Work to completion of row 46.
Cast (bind) off.
Rejoin yarn to rem sts at centre front.
**Row 26:** WS facing, purl.
**Row 27:** Knit to last 3 sts, s1, k1,
psso, k1.
Cont decs as set and work to match
first side.

### Trim
Using A, pick up 3 sts in every 4 rows
around ankle.
Cast (bind) off.

### Second shoe
Make second shoe to match.

### Finishing
Join heel seam, pin to heel end of sole.
Carefully pin upper to sole, easing any
excess around toe area, and stitch into
position. Weave in any loose ends.

# Stripy shoes

These shoes can be knitted in a wide range of colourways, and plaited ties will help to keep them firmly attached to a tot's tootsies.

## Size
To fit baby of 3–6 months

## Materials
50g balls of 4ply (sport-weight) 100% cotton yarn: 1 x dark blue (M) and 1 x light blue (C)
Pair of 2.75mm (US 2) needles

## Tension (gauge)
28 sts and 38 rows = 10cm (4in) square over st st using 2.75mm (US 2) needles.

## Abbreviations
See pages 10–11.

## US terms
Moss stitch = seed stitch (see page 10).

## First shoe
### Sole
Using M, cast on 24 sts and work in moss st.
Inc each end of rows 2, 4, 6 and 8. (32 sts)

Work 3 rows. Dec each end of rows 12, 14, 16 and 18. (24 sts)
**Row 19:** Moss st to end, cast on 8 sts.

### Upper
**Row 1:** Using C, knit.
**Row 2:** Inc, purl to end.
**Rows 3–4:** Using M, as rows 1–2.
**Row 5–8:** As rows 1–4.
**Rows 9–10:** As rows 1–2.
**Row 11:** Using C, cast (bind) off 21 sts, using M, k16.
**Row 12:** Inc, p15.
**Row 13:** Using C, k17.
**Row 14:** P17.
**Row 15–16:** Using M, as rows 13–14.
**Rows 17–24:** As rows 13–16 three times.
**Row 25–26:** As rows 13–14.
**Row 27:** As row 15.
**Row 28:** P2tog, p15, cast on 21 sts.
**Row 29:** Using C, knit.
**Row 30:** P2tog, purl to end.
**Rows 31–38:** Work in stripy patt, dec beg of each purl row.
**Row 39:** Cast (bind) off.

## Edging

With RS facing and using M, pick up 21 sts from heel to front, 10 sts across stripes and 21 sts from front to heel.

**Row 1:** Moss 12, cast (bind) off 1, moss 7, dec, moss 8, dec, moss 7, cast (bind) off 1, moss 12.

**Row 2:** Moss 12, yo, moss 24, yo, moss 12.

**Row 3:** Cast (bind) off.

## Make ties

Cut three 46cm (18in) lengths of M and thread halfway through an eyelet. With one end from each side of eyelet – two strands for each section – plait to end and knot. Trim ends.

## Second shoe

Make second shoe to match.

## Finishing

Join heel seam. Carefully fit upper to sole, easing fullness around toe area, and stitch into position. Weave in loose ends.

# Heel and toe socks

**A classic sock design that looks fabulous in any colourway, these tiny socks are a perfect gift for any baby.**

## Size
To fit baby of 3–6 months

## Materials
### Pink colourway
50g balls of 4ply (sport-weight) 100% wool yarn: 1 x mid-pink (M) and 1 x dark pink (C)

### Blue colourway
50g balls of 4ply (sport-weight) 100% wool yarn: 1 x mid-blue (M) and 1 x dark blue (C)

4 double-pointed 3mm (US 2) needles

## Tension (gauge)
28 sts and 38 rows = 10cm (4in) square over st st using 3mm (US 2) needles.

## Abbreviations
See pages 10–11.

## First sock
Note: place marker at beginning of round.

## Cuff
Using M, cast on 32 sts (10, 10 and 12 sts). Work 5 rounds in *k1, p1* to end.
**Rounds 7–20:** *K3, p1* to end.
DO NOT BREAK M, join in C.

## Start heel
**Round 21:** Using C, k15, turn, leave rem sts on needles for instep.
On 15 sts, work 7 rows in st st, starting with a purl row.

## Shape heel
**Row 1:** K9, turn.
**Row 2:** S1, p2, turn.
**Row 3:** S1, k1, s1, k1, psso, k1, turn.
**Row 4:** S1, p2, p2tog, p1, turn.
**Row 5:** S1, k3, s1, k1, psso, k1, turn.
**Row 6:** S1, p4, p2tog, p1, turn.
**Row 7:** S1, k5, s1, k1, psso, turn.
**Row 8:** S1, p6, p2tog, p1.

Break yarn.
Using M, pick up and knit 6 sts along heel, 9 sts from needle, 6 sts along heel, *p1, k3* four times from instep, move round marker to here and last st to left-hand needle.

Cont as folls:
**Round 1:** P2tog, k19, p2tog, *k3, p1* three times, k3.
**Round 2:** P2tog, k17, p2tog, *k3, p1* three times, k3.
**Round 3:** P2tog, k15, p2tog, *k3, p1* three times, k3.
**Round 4:** P2tog, k13, p2tog, *k3, p1* three times, k3.
**Round 5:** P1, k13, *p1, k3* four times.
**Rounds 6–24:** As round 5.
Break M.

## Shape toe
Using C,
**Round 1:** Knit.
**Round 2:** *K2tog, k11, s1, k1, psso* twice.
**Round 3:** Knit.
**Round 4:** *K2tog, k9, s1, k1, psso* twice.
**Round 5:** Knit.
**Round 6:** *K2tog, k7, s1, k1, psso* twice.
**Round 7:** Knit.
**Round 8:** Cast (bind) off.

## Second sock
Make second sock to match.

## Finishing
Join toe seam (see page 8). Weave in any loose ends.

# Polka-dot shoes

These comic-book shoes make the most of a tiny girl's toes. Red and white is a classic colour combination, but these also look good in complementary colourways; try blue and yellow, for example.

## Size
To fit baby of 6–9 months

## Materials
50g ball of 4ply (sport-weight)
  100% mercerized cotton yarn:
  1 x red (M)
Small amount of white yarn (C)
Pair of 3mm (US 2) needles
2 small buttons

## Tension (gauge)
26 sts and 32 rows = 10cm (4in) square
  over Fair Isle using 3mm (US 2)
  needles.

## Abbreviations
See pages 10–11.

## First shoe
### Sole
Using M, cast on 42 sts.
**Row 1:** K1, inc, k16, inc, k4, inc, k16, inc, k1.
**Row 2 & alt rows:** Knit.
**Row 3:** K2, inc, k17, inc, k4, inc, k17, inc, k2.
**Row 5:** K3, inc, k18, inc, k4, inc, k18, inc, k3.
**Row 7:** K4, inc, k19, inc, k4, inc, k19, inc, k4.
**Row 9:** K5, inc, k20, inc, k4, inc, k20, inc, k5. (62 sts)

### Side of shoe
Change to st st.
**Row 1:** M.
**Row 2:** *2C, 4M* to last 2 sts, 2C.
**Rows 3–4:** 3C, *2M, 4C* to last 5 sts, 2M, 3C.
**Row 5:** As row 2.
**Row 6:** M.
**Row 7:** 3M, *2C, 4M* to last 5 sts, 2C, 3M.
**Rows 8–9:** 2M, *4C, 2M* to end.
**Row 10:** As row 7.

### Start instep

**Row 11:** Using M, k35, s1, k1, psso, turn.

**Row 12:** S1, 3M, 2C, 3M, p2tog, turn.

**Row 13:** S1, 2M, 4C, 2M, s1, k1, psso, turn.

**Row 14:** S1, 2M, 4C, 2M, p2tog, turn.

**Row 15:** S1, 3M, 2C, 3M, s1, k1, psso, turn.

**Row 16:** S1, 8M, p2tog, turn.

**Row 17:** S1, 8M, s1, k1, psso, turn.

**Row 18:** As row 16.

**Rows 19–22:** As rows 17–18 twice.

**Row 23:** S1, k8, s1, k1, psso, k19.

**Row 24:** K28, k2tog, knit 19.

**Row 25:** Cast (bind) off.

### Ankle strap

Join heel and under-foot seam. Weave in any loose ends.

Cast on 7 sts, with RS facing, pick up and knit 14 sts from heel (7 sts from each side of heel seam), cast on 7 sts.

**Row 1:** Knit.

**Row 2:** Knit to last 4 sts, k2tog, yo, k2.

**Row 3:** Knit.

**Row 4:** Cast (bind) off.

### Bow

Cast on 20 sts. Knit 13 rows. Cast (bind) off.

### Second shoe

Make second shoe to match.

### Finishing

Stitch ends of bow together and fold in half with seam at centre back. Run a gathering thread vertically through centre of bow and pull tight, then wrap yarn several times around centre of the bow to cover gathering thread. Stitch bow to front of shoe (see photograph on page 69). Stitch on buttons (see page 8).

# Textured cuff bootees

**Wool and cotton mix yarn is great for baby boots; the warmth of wool keeps feet snug while the crispness of cotton shows up textured stitches.**

## Size
To fit baby of 3–6 months

## Materials
50g ball of 4ply (sport-weight)
  wool and cotton blend yarn:
  1 x cream
Pair each of 3.25mm (US 3) and US 6
  (4mm) needles

## Tension (gauge)
22 sts and 30 rows = 10cm (4in) square
  over st st using 4mm (US 6) needles.

## Abbreviations
See pages 10–11.

## US terms
Moss stitch = seed stitch
  (see page 10).

## First bootee
### Cuff
Using 4mm (US 6) needles, cast on
27 sts and work 10 rows in moss st.
Change to 3.25mm (US 3) needles and
work 6 rows in k1, p1 rib.
Change to 4mm (US 6) needles and st
st and work 4 rows.

### Divide for top of foot
K18, turn, p9, turn.
On 9 sts, work 12 rows st st.
Break yarn.
With RS facing (9 sts on needle), pick
up 10 sts along side of foot, 9 sts from
toe, 10 sts along side of foot and 9 sts
on needle. (47 sts)
Work 6 rows in st st, starting with a
purl row.

### Shape sole
**Row 7:** Knit.
**Row 8:** K1, p2tog, *k1, p1* eight times,
k1, p2tog, k1, p1, k1, p2tog, *k1, p1* eight
times, k1, p2tog, k1.

**Row 9:** *K1, p1* to last st, k1.

**Row 10:** K1, k2tog, moss 15, p2tog, k1, p1, k1, p2tog, moss 15, k2tog, k1.

**Row 11:** K1, moss 16, *p1, k1* twice, p1, moss 16, k1.

**Row 12:** K1, p2tog, moss 13, p2tog, k1, p1, k1, p2tog, moss 13, p2tog, k1.

**Row 13:** As row 9.

**Row 14:** Cast (bind) off.

## Second bootee

Make second bootee to match.

## Finishing

Join leg seam and under-foot seam (see page 8). Weave in any loose ends.

# Bobble shoes

Colourful, fun and tactile, babies will love these jolly shoes. Be sure to sew the bobbles on securely so that little fingers can't cause trouble.

## Size
To fit baby of 3–6 months

## Materials
50g ball of DK (light worsted)
    100% wool yarn: 1 x navy
Small amounts of bright colours for
    bobbles
Pair each of 3mm (US 2) and 4mm
    (US 6) needles

## Tension (gauge)
26 sts and 36 rows = 10cm (4in) square
    over st st using 3mm (US 2) needles.

## Abbreviations
See pages 10–11.

## First shoe
### Sole
Start at heel end. Using of 3mm
(US 2) needles, cast on 3 sts and work

in moss (seed) st. Inc each end of rows 2, 3, 5, 6 and 8. (13 sts)

Cont without shaping to completion of row 36. Dec each end of next and every alt row to 5 sts.

**Next row:** Purl.

Change to st st and work as folls (shaping rows only given):

## Upper

**Row 1:** Inc in 2 sts, k1, inc in 2 sts. (9 sts)

**Row 3:** *K1, inc in next 2 sts, k1* twice, k1. (13 sts)

**Row 5:** *K2, inc in next 2 sts, k2* twice, k1. (17 sts)

**Row 7:** K3, inc, k8, inc, k4. (19 sts)

**Row 10:** *P2, inc* twice, p6, *inc, p2* twice, p1. (23 sts)

**Row 25:** K10, cast (bind) off 3 sts, k10. On 10 sts:

**Row 27:** K1, k2tog, k7.

**Row 29:** K1, k2tog, k6.

**Row 31:** K1, k2tog, k5. (7 sts)

**Row 45:** Cast (bind) off.

Rejoin yarn to rem sts at centre front.

**Row 27:** K7, s1, k1, psso, k1.

Cont decs as set and work to match first side.

## Edging

Using a bright colour and 3mm (US 2) needles, pick up and knit 35 sts around ankle.

Cast (bind) off.

## Bobbles

Make as many different coloured bobbles as you want for each shoe – we made eight for each one.

Using 4mm (US 6) and a bright colour, cast on 3 sts leaving a 10cm (4in) end for Finishing.

**Row 1:** Inc, inc, k1.

**Row 2:** Purl.

**Row 3:** Knit.

**Row 4:** Purl.

**Row 5:** S1, k1, psso, k1, k2tog.

**Row 6:** P3tog.

**Row 7:** Fasten off, leaving a 10cm (4in) end for Finishing.

Tie the two ends together tightly to make a bobble.

## Second shoe

Make second shoe to match.

## Finishing

Join heel seam, pin to heel end of sole. Carefully pin upper to sole, easing any excess around toe area, and stitch into position. Weave in any loose ends. Using loose ends, stitch bobbles randomly to shoe (see page 8).

# Duck feet

Quack-quack, here comes a little duck. These are here to make you laugh, though a firm cuff makes them practical, too.

## Size
To fit baby of 3–6 months

## Materials
50g ball of 4ply (sport-weight)
   100% mercerized cotton yarn:
   1 x yellow
Small amount of orange yarn
Pair of 3.25mm (US 3) needles

## Tension (gauge)
24 sts and 36 rows = 10cm (4in) square
   over st st using 3.25mm (US 3)
   needles.

## Abbreviations
See pages 10–11.

## First foot
### Sole
Cast on 3 sts. Working in moss st, inc each end of rows 2, 3, 5 and 7. (11 sts)
Inc each end of rows 13, 19, 25, 31, 37 and 43. (23 sts)
Work to completion of row 48.

### Upper
Change to st st and work 24 rows.
**Row 25:** K10, cast (bind) off 3 sts, k10.
On 10 sts:
**Row 26:** Purl.
**Row 27:** K1, k2tog, knit to end.
**Rows 28–31:** As rows 26–27 twice. (7 sts)
Work 13 more rows.
Cast (bind) off.
Rejoin yarn to rem sts at centre edge.
**Row 26:** Purl.
**Row 27:** Knit to last 3 sts, s1, k1, psso, k1.
Work to match first side.

## Cuff

With RS facing, pick up 36 sts around ankle. Work 26 rows in k2, p2 rib. Cast (bind) off.

## Second foot

Make second foot to match.

## Finishing

Join cuff and heel seam. Join upper to sole. Weave in any loose ends. Blanket stitch across toe ends of feet using orange.

# Simple shoes

A wonderfully easy design to knit, these shoes can be embellished in dozens of different ways to co-ordinate with any outfit or to suit any occasion.

## Size
To fit baby of 3–6 months

## Materials
**Rose shoe**
50g ball of 4ply (sport-weight)
   100% cotton yarn: 1 x pale green
Silk rose and bow

**Sequin shoe**
50g ball of 4ply (sport-weight)
   100% cotton yarn: 1 x purple
Sequin strip and heart motif

**Watermelon shoe**
50g ball of 4ply (sport-weight)
   100% cotton yarn: 1 x pale pink
Pink, green and black embroidery thread

**Star shoe**
50g ball of 4ply (sport-weight)
   100% cotton yarn: 1 x pale blue
Blue embroidery thread

Pair of 2.75mm (US 2) needles
Safety pin (for stitch holder)
2 small buttons

## Tension (gauge)
28 sts and 38 rows = 10cm (4in)
   square over st st using 2.75mm
   (US 2) needles.

## Abbreviations
See pages 10–11.

## US terms
Moss stitch = seed stitch
   (see page 10).

## Right shoe
### Sole
Cast on 24 sts and work in moss st.
Inc each end of rows 2, 4, 6 and 8.
(32 sts)
Work 3 rows. Dec each end of rows 12,
14, 16 and 18. (24 sts)
**Row 19:** Moss to end, cast on 8 sts.

### Upper
**Row 1:** Knit.
**Row 2:** Inc, purl to end.
**Rows 3–8:** As rows 1–2 three times.
**Row 9:** Knit.
**Row 10:** Inc, p14, moss 21.
**Row 11:** Moss 21, k16.
**Row 12:** Inc, p15, moss 21. (38 sts)
**Row 13:** Cast (bind) off 12 sts, moss 3,
cast (bind) off 4 sts, moss 2, k17.
**Row 14:** P17, moss 2, leave 3 sts on
safety pin.
**Row 15:** Moss 2, k17.
**Rows 16–25:** As rows 14–15 five times.
**Row 26:** P17, moss 2, cast on 19 sts.
**Row 27:** Moss 21, k17.

### 1 Star shoe

So simple a child could do it. The embroidery on this shoe is an arrangement of straight stitches and French knots.

### 2 Rose shoe

Store-bought embellishments really come into their own here. Experiment with different colours and styles.

### 3 Sequin shoe

Glamorous girls will love these sequinned shoes. Choose the brightest colours and co-ordinating buttons.

### 4 Watermelon shoe

Use cotton embroidery thread and simple stitches to embroider a motif onto the toes of a pair of shoes.

**Row 28:** P2tog, p15, moss 21.
**Row 29:** Moss 21, k16.
**Row 30:** P2tog, purl to end.
**Rows 31–38:** Work in st st, dec beg of each purl row.
**Row 39:** Cast (bind) off.

### Strap
Place 3 sts from safety pin onto needle.
**Row 1:** Inc, inc, k1.
**Rows 2–15:** Moss st.
**Row 16:** Moss 2, cast (bind) off 1, moss 2.
**Row 17:** Moss 2, yo, moss 2.
**Rows 18–20:** Moss st.
**Row 21:** Cast (bind) off.

## Left shoe
### Sole
As for right shoe.

### Upper
Rev st st, eg:
**Row 1:** Purl.
**Row 2:** Inc, knit to end.
**Row 10:** Inc, k14, moss 21.

## Finishing
Join heel seam. Carefully fit upper to sole, easing fullness around toe area, and stitch into position. Weave in any loose ends. Stitch on buttons (see page 8).

### Star shoe
Using straight stitch, embroider a star on toe of shoe with French knots at the ends of each stitch (see photograph opposite).

### Rose shoe
Stitch silk rose (available from good haberdashery and craft shops) to front of shoe and bow to heel of shoe.

### Sequin shoe
Stitch sequin strip around rim of shoe and across strap. Stitch sequin heart motif to toe of shoe.

### Watermelon shoe
Using satin stitch, embroider simple watermelon shape (see photograph opposite) on toe of shoe. Add black French knots for seeds.

# Lace and diamond bootees

Classic bootees that combine different textures, these are perfect for a contemporary christening or a wedding as they are pretty, but not too frilly.

## Size
To fit baby of 6–9 months

## Materials
50g ball of 4ply (sport-weight) 100% mercerized cotton yarn:
1 x cream
Pair of 3.25mm (US 3) needles
76cm (30in) of ribbon

## Tension (gauge)
24 sts and 30 rows = 10cm (4in) square over st st using 3.25mm (US 3) needles.

## Abbreviations
See pages 10–11.

## First bootee
### Cuff
Cast on 49 sts.
**Row 1:** *K1, yo, k4, s1, k2tog, psso, k4, yo* four times, k1.
**Row 2 & alt rows:** Purl.
**Row 3:** *K2, yo, k3, s1, k2tog, psso, k3, yo, k1* four times, k1.
**Row 5:** *K3, yo, k2, s1, k2tog, psso, k2, yo, k2* four times, k1.
**Row 7:** *K4, yo, k1, s1, k2tog, psso, k1, yo, k3* four times, k1.
**Row 9:** *K5, s1, k2tog, psso, k4* four times, k1. (41 sts)
**Row 10:** *P2tog, p8* four times, p1. (37 sts)
Change to k1, p1 rib, work 7 rows.
**Next row:** K1, *k1, yo, k2tog* to end.
Change to st st. Work 3 rows, starting with a purl row.

### Divide for top of foot
K25, turn, p13, turn.
On 13 sts, work 4 rows in st st.
**Row 5:** K6, p1, k6.
**Row 6:** P5, k3, p5.
**Row 7:** K4, p5, k4.
**Row 8:** P3, k7, p3.
**Row 9:** K2, p9, k2.
**Row 10:** As row 8.
**Row 11:** As row 7.
**Row 12:** As row 6.

**Row 13:** As row 5.
**Rows 14–16:** St st. Break yarn.
With RS facing (12 sts on needle), pick up and knit 13 sts along side of foot, 13 sts from toe, 13 sts from side of foot and 12 sts from needle. (63 sts) Knit 11 rows.

## Shape sole

**Row 1:** *K1, k2tog, k26, k2tog* twice, k1.
**Row 2:** K1, k2tog, knit to last 3 sts, k2tog, k1.
**Row 3:** *K1, k2tog, k23, k2tog* twice, k1.
**Row 4:** As row 2.
**Row 5:** *K1, k2tog, k20, k2tog* twice, k1.
**Row 6:** Cast (bind) off.

## Second bootee

Make second bootee to match.

## Finishing

Join leg seam and under foot seam. Weave in any loose ends. Cut ribbon in half, thread through eyelets and tie in bow (see page 8).

# Entrelac socks

These socks are have entrelac cuffs and are a more challenging design for the experienced knitter to try.

## Size
To fit baby of 3–6 months

## Materials
50g balls of 4ply (sport-weight) 100% wool yarn: 1 x cream (M) and 1 x red (C)
Pair of 3mm (US 2) needles

## Tension (gauge)
28 sts and 38 rows = 10cm (4in) square over st st using 3mm (US 2) needles.

## Abbreviations
See pages 10–11.

## US terms
Moss stitch = seed stitch (see page 10).

## First sock
### Cuff
Using C, cast on 56 sts and knit 1 row. Start entrelac.

**Row 1:** K3, s1, k1, psso, turn, p4.
◆ **Rows 2–3:** As row 1.
**Row 4:** *K3, s1, k1, psso* twice, turn, p4. ◆

Rep ◆ to ◆ along row, casting (binding) off 4 sts at end of last repeat. With WS facing and using M, pick up 4 sts purlwise along A (see fig. 1, page 86), turn, k4.

*Rows 1–3:** P3, p2tog, turn, k4.*
**Row 4:** P3, p2tog, pick up 4 sts purlwise along A (see fig. 1, page 86), turn, k4.*

Rep * to * along row. Work 5 rows st st on last 4 sts. Cast (bind) off. With RS facing and using C, pick up 4 sts along B (see fig. 2, page 86), turn, p4.

◆ **Rows 1–3:** K3, s1, k1, psso, turn, p4.
**Row 4:** *K3, s1, k1, psso* twice, turn, p4. ◆

Rep ◆ to ◆ along row. Work 6 rows in st st on last 4 sts. Break C.

WS facing, using M *p4, pick up 3 sts along a (see fig. 1, below)* to end. (49 sts)

**Next row:** *K2, k2tog, k3* to end. (42 sts)

### Start rib patt

**Row 1:** WS facing *k1, p4, k1* to end.
**Row 2:** *P1, k4, p1* to end.
**Row 3:** *K1, p1, k2, p1, k1* to end.
**Row 4:** *P1, k1, p2, k1, p1* to end.
**Rows 5–16:** As rows 1–4 three times.
**Row 17:** As row 1. Break M.

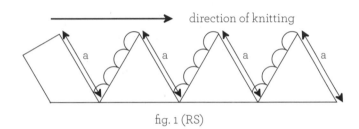

fig. 1 (RS)

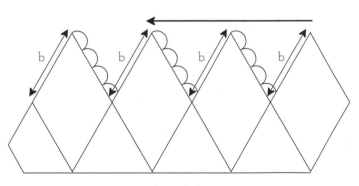

fig. 2 (RS)

## Work instep

Slip 13 sts, using M, *k4, p2* twice, k4, turn.
On 16 sts, work 19 rows in patt.
Break M.

## Work toe

Using C, k2, k2tog, k3, k2tog, k3, s1, k1, psso, k2. (13 sts)
Work 3 rows in moss st (every row *k1, p1* to last st, k1). Dec each end of next and foll 4th row. (9 sts)
Work 3 rows. Break C.

## Work heel and foot

Slip all sts onto 1 needle, RS facing, using C, k13, pick up and knit 11 sts along instep, 6 sts along toe, moss 9 sts from needle, pick up and knit 6 sts along toe, 11 sts along instep, k13 sts from needle. (69 sts)
Work in moss st, shaping rows only given.

**Row 5:** Moss 27, p3tog, moss 9, p3tog, moss 27.
**Row 9:** Moss 26, s1, k2tog, psso, moss 7, s1, k2tog, psso, moss 26.
**Row 13:** Moss 25, p3tog, moss 5, p3tog, moss 25.
**Row 16:** Moss 2, *s1, k2tog, psso, moss 19, s1, k2tog, psso*, moss 3, *to* again, moss 2.
**Row 18:** *K1, p3tog, moss 17, p3tog* twice, k1.

## Second sock

Make second sock to match.

## Finishing

Join leg and under-foot seam (see page 9). Weave in any loose ends.

# Fair Isle shoes

Fair Isle fans will love these ankle-strap shoes, which look good in pastel shades, as well as in the darker, bolder colours shown here.

## Size
To fit baby of 3–6 months

## Materials
50g ball of 4ply (sport-weight) 100% mercerized cotton yarn:
    1 x dark blue (M)
Small amounts of yellow (A), red (B) and green yarn (C)
Pair of 2.75mm (US 2) needles
2 small buttons

## Tension (gauge)
26 sts and 34 rows = 10cm (4in) square over Fair Isle using 2.75mm (US 2) needles.

## Abbreviations
See pages 10–11.

## US terms
Moss stitch = seed stitch (see page 10).

## First bootee
### Sole
Using M, cast on 19 sts and work in moss st.
Inc each end of rows 2, 4 and 6. (25 sts)
Work 2 rows. Dec each end of rows 9, 11 and 13. (19 sts)
**Row 14:** Moss to end, cast on 6 sts. (25 sts)

### Upper
Change to st st and work Fair Isle following instructions and chart (starting with a knit row):
**Row 1:** *1M, 1A* to last st, 1M.
**Row 2:** M inc, purl to end.
**Row 3:** 1M, *1B, 2M, 1C, 2M* to last st, 1B.
**Row 4:** Inc B, *1B, 1C, 1A, 1C, 1B, 1A* to last st, 1B.
**Row 5:** As row 3 to last 2sts, 1B, 1M.
**Row 6**: As row 2.
**Row 7:** *1M, 1A* to end.

**Row 8:** M inc p10, *k1, p1* to last st, k1.

**Row 9:** Moss 18M, knit 1M, 1B, 2M, 1C, 2M, 1B, 2M, 1C.

**Row 10:** Purl inc A, 1C, 1B, 1A, 1B, 1C, 1A, 1C, 1B, 1A, 1B, using M, *p1, k1* to end.

**Row 11:** Cast (bind) off 15 sts, *p1, k1* twice, knit 1B, 2M, 1C, 2M, 1B, 2M, 1C, 1M.

**Row 12:** Using M, p13, k1, p1.

**Row 13:** Using M, *p1, k1* twice, knit *1A, 1M* to last st, 1A.

**Row 14:** As row 12.

**Row 15:** Using M, *p1, k1* twice, knit 1B, 2M, 1C, 2M, 1B, 2M, 1C, 1M.

**Row 16:** Purl *1C, 1A, 1C, 1B, 1A, 1B* twice, using M, p1, k1, p1, cast on 15 sts.

**Row 17:** Moss 18M, knit 1M, 1B, 2M, 1C, 2M, 1B, 2M, 2togC.

- ■ M, knit on RS purl on WS
- ■ M, purl on WS knit on WS
- □ A
- ■ B
- ■ C

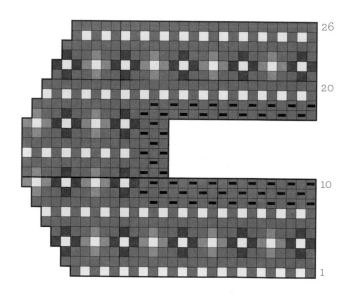

**Row 18:** Using M, p11, moss 18.
**Row 19:** Knit *1M, 1A* to last 3 sts, 1M, 2togA.
**Row 20:** M.
**Row 21:** As row 3 to last 3 sts, 1B, 2togM.
**Row 22:** *1B, 1A, 1B, 1C, 1A, 1C* to last 3 sts, 1B, 1A, 1B.
**Row 23:** As row 3 to last 2 sts, 2togB.
**Row 24:** M.
**Row 25:** *1M, 1A* to last 2 sts, 2togM.
**Row 26:** M.
**Row 27:** Cast (bind) off.

## Second bootee

Make second shoe to match.

## Finishing

Join heel seam. Carefully fit upper to sole, easing fullness around toe area, and stitch into position. Weave in any loose ends.

### Strap

Using M, cast on 8 sts, with RS of shoe facing, pick up and knit 10 sts from heel (5 sts from each side of heel seam), cast on 8 sts. (26 sts)
**Row 1:** *K1, p1* to end.
**Row 2:** *P1, k1* to last 4 sts, p2tog, yo, p1, k1.
**Row 3:** As row 1.
**Row 4:** Cast (bind) off.
Sew on button (see page 8).

# Roll-top bootees

These bootees are a great, simple shape and the modern roll-top edging in a contrast colour complements the simple embellishment.

## Size
To fit baby of 0–3[3–6] months

## Materials
50g ball of 4ply (sport-weight)
    100% wool yarn: 1 x ball of navy (M)
Small amount of red yarn (C)
Pair of 3mm (US 2) needles

## Tension (gauge)
28 sts and 38 rows = 10cm (4in) square
    over st st using 3mm (US 2) needles.

## Abbreviations
See pages 10–11.

## First bootee
### Cuff
Using C, cast on 41 sts and work
10 rows in st st.
Change to M and work 6 rows.
**Row 7:** K2, *yo, k2tog, k2* nine times,
yo, k2tog, k1.
Work 3 more rows.

### Divide for top of foot
K28 turn, p15 turn.
On 15 sts, work 16[22] rows.
Break yarn.
With RS facing (13 sts on needle), rejoin
M and pick up 11[17] sts along side of
foot, 15 sts from toe, 11[17]sts along side

of foot and 13 sts on needle. (63:75 sts)
Knit 13 rows.

### Shape sole
**Row 1:** K1, *k2tog, k25[31], k2tog*, k3,
*to* again, k1.
**Row 2:** K26[32], k2tog, k3, k2tog, k26[32].
**Row 3:** K1, *k2tog, k22[28], k2tog*, k3,
*to* again, k1.
**Row 4:** K23[29], k2tog, k3, k2tog,
k23[29].
**Row 5:** K1, *k2tog, k19[25], k2tog*, k3,
*to* again, k1.
**Row 6:** Cast (bind) off.

### Make ties
Using C, cut six 46cm (18in) lengths of
yarn. Knot together at one end. With
two strands for each section, plait to
end and knot to secure.

## Second bootee
Make second bootee to match.

## Finishing
Join leg seam and under-foot seam.
Weave in any loose ends. Make French
knots around garter stitch edge and
embroider straight stitch star on toe
(see photograph). Thread ties through
eyelets and tie in bow (see page 8).

# Tiger bootees

Stylish bootees for wild little ones. Cool cotton yarn makes them comfortable in summer, as well as fashionable.

## Size
To fit baby of 3-6 months

## Materials
50g balls of 4ply (sport-weight) 100% cotton yarn: 1 x black (A) and 1 x yellow (B)
Pair of 2.75mm (US 2) needles

## Tension (gauge)
26 sts and 34 rows = 10cm (4in) square over st st using 2.75mm (US 2) needles.

## Abbreviations
See pages 10–11.

## First bootee
### Sole
Start at heel end. Using A, cast on 3 sts and work in moss st. Inc each end of rows 2, 3, 5, 6 and 8. (13 sts)
Cont without shaping to completion of row 36. Dec each end of next and every alt row to 5 sts.
**Next row:** Purl.

### Upper
**Row 1:** Using B, inc in 2 sts, k1, inc in 2 sts. (9 sts)
**Row 2:** Purl.
**Row 3:** K1, *inc in next 2 sts, k2* twice. (13 sts)
**Row 4:** Purl.
Cont in st st.
**Row 5:** K2, inc in next 2 sts, k4, inc in next 2 sts, k3. (17 sts)
**Row 6:** 3A, 11B, 3A.
**Row 7:** 2A, inc A, 3A, 5B, 3A, inc A, 2A. (19 sts)
**Row 8:** 6A, 7B, 6A.
**Row 9:** 2A, 15B, 2A.

**Row 10:** Using B, *p2, inc* twice, p6, *inc, p2* twice, p1. (23 sts)

**Row 11:** Work tiger patt following instructions and chart: B.

**Row 12:** 4A, 15B, 4A.

**Row 13:** 10A, 3B, 10A.

**Row 14:** 8A, 7B, 8A.

**Row 15:** 4A, 15B, 4A.

**Rows 16–17:** B.

**Row 18:** 1A, 21B, 1A.

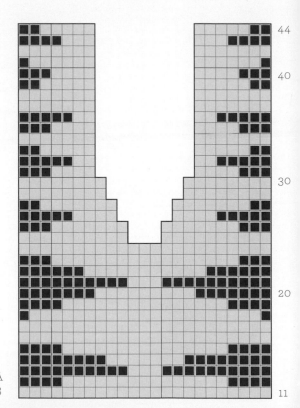

A
B

**Row 19:** 4A, 15B, 4A.
**Row 20:** 7A, 9B, 7A.
**Row 21:** 10A, 3B, 10A.
**Row 22:** 6A, 11B, 6A.
**Row 23:** 3A, 17B, 3A.
**Row 24:** B.
**Row 25:** 10B, cast (bind) off 3 sts, 10B.
On 10 sts:
**Row 26:** 3A, 7B.
**Row 27:** 1B, 2togB, 2B, 5A.
**Row 28:** 2A, 7B.
**Row 29:** 1B, 2togB, 6B.
**Row 30:** B.
**Row 31:** 1B, 2togB, 2B, 3A. (7 sts)
**Row 32:** 5A, 2B.
**Row 33:** 5B, 2A.
**Row 34:** B.
**Row 35:** 4B, 3A.
**Row 36:** 5A, 2B.
**Rows 37–38:** B.
**Row 39:** 5B, 2A.
**Row 40:** 3A, 4B.
**Row 41:** 6B, 1A.
**Row 42:** B.

**Row 43:** 3B, 4A.
**Row 44:** 2A, 5B.
**Row 45:** Cast (bind) off.
Rejoin yarn to rem sts at centre front.
**Row 26:** WS facing, 7B, 3A.
**Row 27:** 5A, 2B, s1, 1B, psso, 1B.
Cont decs as set and work to match
first side.

### Cuff
With RS facing and using A, pick up
35 sts around ankle.
Work 26 rows in k1, p1 rib.
WS facing, change to B and knit 1 row.
Cast (bind) off.

### Second bootee
Make second bootee to match.

### Finishing
Join cuff and heel seam, pin to heel
end of sole. Carefully pin upper to sole,
easing any excess around toe area,
and stitch into position. Weave in any
loose ends.

# Star bootees

A simple design and an equally easy intarsia motif make these a good project for a knitting beginner.

## Size
To fit baby of 6–9 months

## Materials
50g ball of 4ply (sport-weight)
    100% wool yarn: 1 x dark blue (M)
Small amounts of yellow (C) and
    green yarn
Pair of 3mm (US 2) needles

## Tension (gauge)
28 sts and 38 rows = 10cm (4in) square
    over st st using 3mm (US 2) needles.

## Abbreviations
See pages 10–11.

## First bootee
### Cuff
Using M, cast on 41 sts and work 2cm (¾in) in garter st. Change to st st, work 2 rows.
**Row 3:** K2, *yo, k2tog, k2* nine times, yo, k2tog, k1.
Work 3 more rows.

## Divide for top of foot
K28 turn, p15, turn.
On 15 sts, work 8 rows.
**Row 9:** Place star motif following chart: knit 7M, 1C, 7M.
Work star motif then work 4 more rows (toe), break yarn.
With RS facing (13 sts on needle), rejoin M and pick up and knit 16 sts along side of foot, 15 sts from toe, 16 sts along side of foot and 13 sts on needle. (73 sts)
Knit 13 rows.

## Shape sole
Using M,
**Row 1:** K1, *k2tog, k30, k2tog*, k3, *to* again, k1.
**Row 2:** K31, k2tog, k3, k2tog, k31.
**Row 3:** K1, *k2tog, k27, k2tog*, k3, *to* again, k1.
**Row 4:** K28, k2tog, k3, k2tog, k28.
**Row 5:** K1, *k2tog, k24, k2tog*, k3, *to* again, k1.
**Row 6:** Cast (bind) off.

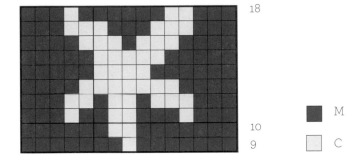

18

10
9

■ M

☐ C

## Second bootee

Make second bootee to match.

## Finishing

Join leg seam and under-foot seam. Weave in any loose ends. Plait three lengths of green yarn together to make ties, knotting ends to secure them. Thread ties through eyelets and tie in bow (see page 8).

# Chunky ankle-strap shoes

These little shoes knit up very quickly and show off the thickness of the yarn. The wooden buttons add to the rustic feel.

## Size
To fit baby of 6–9 months

## Materials
100g ball of aran (worsted) weight wool and alpaca blend: 1 x blue
Pair of 4mm (US 6) needles
2 small buttons

## Tension (gauge)
20 sts and 38 rows = 10cm (4in) over garter st using 4mm (US 6) needles.

## Abbreviations
See pages 10–11.

## First shoe
### Sole
Cast on 14 sts. Working in garter st, inc each end of rows 2, 4 and 6.
Work row 7. Dec each end of rows 8, 10 and 12.
Cast (bind) off.

### Upper
Cast on 19 sts. Working in garter st, inc beg of rows 2, 4, 6, 8 and 10 (toe end).
**Row 11:** Cast (bind) off 11 sts, knit to end.
**Rows 12–26:** Knit.
**Row 27:** Cast on 11 sts, k24.
Dec beg rows 28, 30, 32, 34 and 36.
Cast (bind) off.

### Strap
Join heel seam on upper. Cast on 10sts, pick up and knit 10 sts from back of shoe (5 sts each side of heel seam), cast on 10 sts.
Knit 1 row.
**Row 2:** Knit to last 3 sts, cast (bind) off 1 st, k2.
**Row 3:** K2, yo, knit to end.
**Row 4:** Knit.
**Row 5:** Cast (bind) off.

## Second shoe
Make second shoe to match.

## Finishing

Pin heel seam to centre of shaped edge of sole and cast-on and cast-off (bound-off) edges of sole end to shoe upper. Run a thread through shaped toe of upper and pull tight until upper fits the shaped (toe) end of sole. Stitch around sole. Weave in any loose ends. Stitch on buttons (see page 8).

# Contrast-edge slippers

These are ideal for a younger baby as they are easy to put on and a fluffy yarn makes them soft and warm.

## Size
To fit baby of 0–3 months

## Materials
### Pink and green
50g ball of DK (light worsted) mohair and lambswool blend: 1 x pink (M)
Small amount of green yarn (C)

### Green and navy
50g ball of DK (light worsted) mohair and lambswool blend: 1 x green (M)
Small amount of navy yarn (C)

Pair of 4mm (US 6) needles

## Tension (gauge)
22 sts and 40 rows = 10cm (4in) over garter st (every row knit) using 4mm (US 6) needles.

## Abbreviations
See pages 10–11.

## First slipper
### Sole
Using M, cast on 14 sts. Working in garter st, inc each end of rows 1, 3, 5 and 7. (22 sts)
Dec each end of rows 9, 11, 13 and 15. (14 sts)

### Upper
**Row 16:** Cast on 5 sts (for heel), k19. Inc beg rows (toe) 17, 19, 21 and 23. (23 sts)
**Row 24:** Cast (bind) off 12 sts, knit to end.
**Rows 25–35:** Knit.
**Row 36:** Cast on 12 sts, k23.
Dec beg rows 37, 39, 41 and 43. (19 sts)
Cast (bind) off.

### Trim
Using C, pick up and knit 12 sts from heel to centre front, 6s ts from centre front and 12 sts from centre front to heel. Cast (bind) off.

## Second slipper
Make second slipper to match.

## Finishing
Join heel seam. Pin upper around sole, easing excess material around toe, and stitch into position. Weave in any loose ends.

# Stripy bootees

These are great bootees. Not only do they keep a baby's feet warm and snug, but the long, ribbed cuffs mean that they will stay on the most active feet. So if you have a particularly wriggly baby, try knitting this design.

## Size
To fit baby of 3–6[6–9] months

## Materials
### Dark blue colourway
50g balls of DK (light worsted) 100% wool yarn: 1 x dark blue (M) and 1 x cream (C)

### Dark pink colourway
50g balls of DK (light worsted) 100% wool yarn: 1 x dark pink (M) and 1 x cream (C)

### Mid blue colourway
50g balls of DK (light worsted) 100% wool yarn: 1 x mid blue (M) and 1 x cream (C)

### Pale pink colourway
50g balls of DK (light worsted) 100% wool yarn: 1 x pale pink (M) and 1 x cream (C)

Pair of 3.25mm (US 3) needles

## Tension (gauge)
26 sts and 40 rows = 10cm (4in) square over garter st using 3.25mm (US 3) needles.

## Abbreviations
See pages 10–11.

## Sole
Using M, cast on 43[53]sts.
**Row 1:** *Inc, k19[24], inc* twice, k1.
**Rows 2–4:** Knit.
**Row 5:** *Inc, k21[26], inc* twice, k1.
**Rows 6–8:** Knit.
**Row 9:** *Inc, k23[28], inc* twice, k1.
**Row 10:** Knit.

## Picot edge
Change to C.
**Row 1:** Knit.
**Row 2:** Purl.
**Row 3:** K1, *yo, k2tog* to end.
**Row 4:** Purl.
**Rows 5–6:** As rows 1–2.
Change to M.

**Row 7:** Fold work at row of holes and knit together, 1 st from needle and 1 st from FIRST row of picot, all across row.
**Rows 8–16[20]:** Knit.

### Divide for top of foot
**Row 1:** Using M, k31[36], s1, k1, psso, turn.
**Row 2:** Using M, k8, k2tog, turn.
**Row 3:** Using C, k8, s1, k1, psso, turn.
**Row 4:** Using C, k8, k2tog, turn.
**Rows 5–6:** Using M, as rows 3–4.
**Rows 7–18[22]:** As rows 3–6.
Work rows 3–4 again.
**Next row:** Using M, k9, knit to end.
Knit 3 rows across all sts.

### Cuff
Change to k1, p1 rib.
**Rows 1–8:** M.
**Row 9:** Knit in C.
**Rows 10–28:** Still in C, work in k1, p1 rib.
**Row 29:** Purl in M.
Cast (bind) off in M.

### Second bootee
Make second bootee to match.

### Finishing
Join seam using a flat seam (see page 9). Weave in any loose ends.

# Cable socks

The simple shape of this design shows off the cabling beautifully and makes it a great project for knitters who prefer single colour work.

## Size

To fit baby of 3-6 months

## Materials

50g ball of 4ply (sport-weight)
   100% wool yarn: 1 x cream
Pair of 3mm (US 2) needles
Cable needle

## Tension (gauge)

28 sts and 38 rows = 10cm (4in) square
   over st st using 3mm (US 2) needles.

## Abbreviations

**C4b** = slip 2 sts onto cable needle
   and hold at back of work, k2 from
   left hand needle, then k2 from
   cable needle.
See also pages 10-11.

## First sock

### Cuff

Cast on 36 sts and work 5 rows in k1,
p1 rib.
**Row 6:** *Rib 3, inc, rib 2* to end.
(42 sts)
Patt as folls:
**Row 1:** *K4, p3* to end.
**Row 2:** *K2tog, yo, k1, p4* to end.
**Row 3:** *C4b, p3* to end.
**Row 4:** *K3, p4* to end.
**Row 5:** As row 1.
**Row 6:** As row 4.
**Rows 7-24:** As rows 1-6 three times.
**Rows 25-27:** As rows 1-3.

### Divide for instep

**Row 28:** Patt 35, turn, patt 18, turn.

### Work instep

On 18 sts, work 22 rows in patt.
**Row 23:** *P1, p2tog, p1, k3* twice, p1,
p2tog, p1. Break yarn. (15 sts)

### Work heel and foot

Put all sts onto one needle.
With RS facing, k1, k2tog, k4, pick up
and knit 20 sts along instep, 15 sts
from needle, 20 sts along instep and
*k4, k2tog, k1* twice, k3 from needle.
(76 sts)

Cont as folls:

**Row 1 and alt rows:** Purl.

**Row 2:** K25, s1, k1, psso, k13, k2tog, k34.

**Row 4:** K25, s1, k1, psso, k11, k2tog, k34.

**Row 6:** K25, s1, k1, psso, k9, k2tog, k34.

**Row 8:** K25, s1, k1, psso, k7, k2tog, k34.

**Row 10:** K2tog, k22, s1, k2tog, psso, k5, k3tog, k22, s1, k2tog, psso, k6, k2tog.

**Row 12:** K2tog, k20, s1, k2tog, psso, k3, k3tog, k20, s1, k2tog, psso, k4, k2tog.

**Row 14:** K2tog, k18, s1, k2tog, psso, k1, k3tog, k18, s1, k2tog, psso, k2, k2tog.

**Row 15:** Purl.

**Row 16:** Cast (bind) off.

## Second sock

Make second sock to match.

## Finishing

Join leg seam; this is NOT centre back.

Carefully pin under-foot seam, using shapings to mark centre heel and toe. Stitch sole seam (see page 9). Weave in any loose ends.

# Tassel shoes

These shoes look great in primary colours and are really easy to knit – a good design for a novice knitter to try.

## Size
To fit baby of 0–3 months

## Materials
50g ball of DK (light worsted) 100% wool yarn: 1 x red

Small amounts of green, blue and yellow yarn

Pair of 4mm (US 6) needles

2 small buttons

## Tension (gauge)
22 sts and 40 rows = 10cm (4in) square over garter st using 4mm (US 6) needles.

## Abbreviations
See pages 10–11.

## First shoe
### Sole
Cast on 32 sts.

**Row 1:** *K1, inc, k12, inc, k1* twice.
**Row 2 & alt rows:** Knit.
**Row 3:** *K1, inc, k14, inc, k1* twice.
**Row 5:** *K1, inc, k16, inc, k1* twice.
**Row 7:** *K1, inc, k18, inc, k1* twice.
**Row 9:** *K1, inc, k20, inc, k1* twice. (52 sts)
**Rows 10–15:** Knit.

### Shape instep
**Row 16:** K30, turn.
**Rows 17–33:** K7, s1, k1, psso, turn. (35 sts)
**Row 34:** K7, s1, k1, psso, k13.
**Rows 35–37:** Knit across all sts.
**Row 38:** Cast (bind) off.

### Ankle strap
Join heel and under-foot seam. Cast on 6 sts, with RS facing pick up and knit 12 sts from heel (6 sts each side of heel seam), cast on 6 sts.

**Row 1:** Knit.
**Row 2:** Knit to last 4sts, k2tog, yo, k2.
**Row 3:** Knit.
**Row 4:** Cast (bind) off.

## Second shoe

Make second shoe to match.

## Finishing

Weave in any loose ends. Cut five
25cm (10in) lengths of blue yarn. Fold
in half and, using a crochet hook, push
folded ends under a stitch approx 1cm
(½in) below centre front. Tuck cut
ends of yarn through loop and pull
tight to make a tassel. Repeat with
green and yellow yarn either side
of blue yarn. Trim cut ends neatly.
Reverse order of colours on second
shoe. Sew on buttons (see page 8).

# Centre cable bootees

The central cable on these bootees is easy to knit and a contrast colour makes the most of the texture.

## Size
To fit baby of 3–6 months

## Materials
50g ball of DK (light worsted)
   100% wool yarn: 1 x mid-blue (M)
Small amount of cream yarn (C)
Pair of 3mm (US 2) needles
Cable needle

## Tension (gauge)
26 sts and 36 rows = 10cm (4in) square
   over st st using 3mm (US 2) needles.

## Abbreviations
**C4b** = slip 2 sts onto cable needle and
   hold at back of work, k2 from left hand
   needle, then k2 from cable needle.
See also pages 10–11.

## First bootee
### Sole
Start at heel end. Using M, cast on
2 sts and work in moss (seed) st. Inc
each end of rows 2, 3, 5, 6 and 8. (12 sts)

Cont without shaping to completion
of row 36. Dec each end of next and
every alt row to 4 sts.
**Next row:** Purl.

### Upper
Change to st st.
**Row 1:** Inc in each st. (8 sts)
**Row 2:** 2M, 4C, 2M.
**Row 3:** *Inc M* twice, 4C, *inc M*
twice. (12 sts)
**Row 4:** 4M, 4C, 4M.
**Row 5:** 1M, *inc M* twice, 1M, c4bC,
1M, *inc M* twice, 1M. (16 sts)
**Row 6:** 6M, 4C, 6M.
**Row 7:** 3M, inc M, 2M, 4C, 2M, inc M,
3M. (18 sts)
**Row 8:** 7M, 4C, 7M.
**Row 9:** 7M, c4bC, 7M.
**Row 10:** *2M, inc M* twice, 1M, 4C, 1M,
*inc M, 2M* twice. (22 sts)
**Rows 11–12:** 9M, 4C, 9M.
**Row 13:** 9M, c4bC, 9M.
**Row 14:** As row 12.
**Rows 15–22:** As rows 11–14 twice.

**Rows 23–24:** As rows 11–12.
**Row 25:** 9M, cast (bind) off 4 sts, 9M.

On 9 sts, using M,
**Row 26:** Purl.
**Row 27:** K1, k2tog, k6.
**Row 28:** Purl.
**Row 29:** K1, k2tog, k5.
**Row 30:** Purl.
**Rows 31–42:** St st.
**Row 43:** Cast (bind) off.
Rejoin yarn to rem sts at centre front.
**Row 26:** Purl.
**Row 27:** K6, s1, k1, psso, k1.
Cont decs as set and work to match
first side.

## Cuff

Using M, pick up and knit 34 sts
around ankle. Work 24 rows in k1, p1
rib. Change to C, knit 1 row.
Cast (bind) off.

## Second bootee

Make second bootee to match.

## Finishing

Join heel seam, pin to heel end of sole.
Carefully pin upper to sole, easing any
excess around toe area, and stitch into
position. Weave in any loose ends.

# Lacy leaf bootees

Pretty and nostalgic, these are lovely bootees for a baby girl. The lace edging complements the leaf pattern.

## Size
To fit baby of 3–6 months

## Materials
50g ball of DK (light worsted)
    100% wool yarn: 1 x pink
Pair of 4mm (US 6) needles
76cm (30in) of ribbon

## Tension (gauge)
22 sts and 30 rows = 10cm (4in) square
    over st st using 4mm (US 6) needles.

## Abbreviations
See pages 10–11.

## First bootee
### Sole
Cast on 27 sts and work as folls:
**Row 1 & alt rows:** Knit.
**Row 2:** *K1, inc, k10, inc* twice, k1.
**Row 4:** *K1, inc, k12, inc* twice, k1.
**Row 6:** *K1, inc, k14, inc* twice, k1.
**Row 8:** *K1, inc, k16, inc* twice, k1.
**Row 10:** *K1, inc, k18, inc* twice, k1. (47 sts)

### Upper
**Rows 11–19:** Knit.

### Shape top of foot
**Row 1:** K28, s1, k1, psso, turn.
**Row 2:** S1, p9, p2tog, turn.
**Row 3:** S1, k9, s1, k1, psso, turn.
**Rows 4–13:** As rows 2–3 five times.
**Row 14:** S1, p9, p2tog, turn. (33 sts)
**Row 15:** S1, k21.
**Row 16:** Purl across all sts.
**Row 17:** Knit.
**Row 18:** Purl.
**Row 19:** Make eyelets, *k1, yo, k2tog* to end.
**Row 20:** Knit.
**Row 21:** Purl.
**Row 22:** Knit.
**Row 23:** P4, *k1, p5* four times, k1, p4.
**Row 24:** K4, *p1, k5* four times, p1, k4.

**Row 25:** P4,*yo, k1, yo, p5* four times, yo, k1, yo, p4.

**Row 26:** K4, *p3, k5* four times, p3, k4.

**Row 27:** P4, (*k1, yo* twice, k1, p5) four times, *k1, yo* twice, k1, p4.

**Row 28:** K4, *p5, k5* four times, p5, k4.

**Row 29:** P4, *k2, yo, k1, yo, k2, p5* four times, k2, yo, k1, yo, k2, p4.

**Row 30:** K4, *p7, k5* four times, p7, k4

**Row 31:** P4, *k2, s1, k2tog, psso, k2, p5* four times, k2, s1, k2tog, psso, k2, p4.

**Row 32:** As row 28.

**Row 33:** P4, *k1, s1, k2tog, psso, k1, p5* four times, k1, s1, k2tog, psso, k1, p4.

**Row 34:** As row 26.

**Row 35:** P4, *yb, s1, k2tog, psso, p5* four times, yb, s1, k2tog, psso, p4.

**Row 36:** Knit.

**Row 37:** Purl.

**Rows 38–39:** Knit.

**Row 40:** Purl.

**Row 41:** K1, *yo, k2tog* to end. ◆

**Row 42:** Purl.

**Row 43:** Knit.

**Row 44:** Cast (bind) off loosely.

## Second bootee

Make second bootee to match.

## Finishing

Join leg and under-foot seam.
Fold top of leg to inside at ◆ holes and slip stitch into position. Weave in any loose ends.

Cut ribbon in half, thread through eyelets and tie in bow (see page 8).

# Tweed bobble slippers

Subtle tweed colours work well with this design, but you could try classic black and white for a pierrot look.

## Size
To fit baby of 0–3 months

## Material
50g balls of DK (light worsted)
    100% tweedy wool yarn: 1 x violet (A)
    and 1 x blue (B)
Pair of 3.25mm (US 3) needles

## Tension (gauge)
24 sts and 32 rows = 10cm (4in) square
    over st st and 3.25mm (US 3) needles.

## Abbreviations
**MB** = k1, yo, k1, yo, k1 into next st, turn,
    p5, turn, k5, turn, p2tog, p1, p2tog,
    turn, k3tog.

See also pages 10–11.

## First slipper
### Sole
Using B, cast on 3 sts, working in seed (moss) st, inc each end of rows 1, 3 and 5.
Cont in seed (moss) st until work measures 8cm (3¼in).
Dec each end of next and every alt row to 3 sts.
Cast (bind) off.

### Upper
Start at toe. Using A, cast on 5 sts and work in st st. Shaping rows only given.
**Row 1:** K1, inc in next 3 sts, k1.
**Row 3:** K1, inc in next 5 sts, k2.
**Row 5:** K3, inc in next 6 sts, k4. (19 sts)
**Row 9:** K9A, using B mb, k9A.
**Rows 13 & 17:** As row 9.
**Row 21:** K8, cast (bind) off 3 sts, k8.
On 8 sts:
**Row 1:** Purl.
**Row 2:** K1, s1, k1, psso, knit to end.
Rep rows 1–2 twice more. (5 sts)
Work 9 more rows.

Cast (bind) off.
Rejoin yarn to rem sts at centre and work to match.
**Row 2:** Knit to last 3 sts, k2tog, k1.

## Second slipper
Make second slipper to match.

## Finishing
Join heel seam. Pin upper to sole, easing any fullness at toe, and stitch into position. Weave in any loose ends.

# Harlequin bootees

Jaunty turned-up toes and colourful pompoms make these ribbed cuff bootees fun as well as functional.

## Size
To fit baby of 6–9 months

## Materials
**Red cuff, red bobble**
50g balls of DK (light worsted) 100% wool yarn: 1 x blue (A), 1 x red (B) and 1 x yellow (C)
2 red bobbles

**Blue cuff, green bobble**
50g balls of DK (light worsted) 100% wool yarn: 1 x red (A), 1 x blue (B) and 1 x yellow (C)
2 green bobbles

**Red cuff, blue bobble**
50g balls of DK (light worsted) 100% wool yarn: 1 x blue (A), 1 x red (B)and 1 x yellow (C)
2 blue bobbles

**Blue cuff, red bobble**
50g balls of DK (light worsted) 100% wool yarn: 1 x red (A), 1 x blue (B) and 1 x yellow (C)
2 red bobbles

Pair of 3.25mm (US 3) needles

## Tension (gauge)
24 sts and 32 rows = 10cm (4in) square over st st using 3.25mm (US 3) needles.

## Abbreviations
**S2** = slip next 2 sts purlwise.
See also pages 10–11.

## First bootee
### Sole
Using A, cast on 41 sts.
**Row 1:** *Inc, k18, inc* twice, k1.
**Rows 2–3:** Knit.
**Row 4:** *Inc, k20, inc* twice, k1.
**Rows 5–6:** Knit.
**Row 7:** *Inc, k22, inc* twice, k1. (53 sts)
**Row 8:** Knit, break A.
**Row 9:** Using C, knit.
**Row 10:** Purl.

**Row 11:** K1, *yo, k2tog* to end.
**Row 12:** Purl.
**Rows 13–14:** As rows 9 –10.
**Row 15:** Make hem, fold work at row of holes and knit together, 1 st from needle and 1 st from row 9, across row.
**Row 16:** K2tog, k51, break C.

### Sides
**Row 17:** Knit 26A, 26B.
**Row 18:** Using B, k24, inc, k1, yf, using A, inc, k25.
**Row 19:** Knit 27A, 27B.
**Row 20:** Using B, k25, inc, k1, yf, using A, inc, k26.
**Rows 21–28:** Inc as set. (64 sts)
**Row 29:** Knit 32A, 16B, turn.
**Row 30:** Using B, s1, k13, inc, k1, yf, using A, inc, k15, turn.
**Row 31:** S1, k16A, k13B, turn.
**Row 32:** Using B, s1, k10, inc, k1, yf, using A, inc, k12, turn.
**Row 33:** S1, k13A, k10B, turn.
**Row 34:** S1, k9B, yf, k10A, turn.
**Row 35:** S1, k9A, k6B, turn.
**Row 36:** S1, k5B, yf, k6A, turn.
**Row 37:** S1, k5A, k2B, turn.
**Row 38:** S1, k1B, yf, k2A, s1, turn.

Break yarns.

**Shape top**
**Row 39:** Using C, k2tog, k2, s1, k1, psso, turn.
**Row 40:** K4, s2, turn.
**Row 41:** K3tog, k2, s1, k2tog, psso, turn.
**Row 42:** K4, s2, turn.
**Rows 43–52:** As rows 41–42 five times.
**Row 53:** K1, k2tog, k2, s1, k1, psso, k1, turn.
**Row 54:** K6, s1, turn.
**Row 55:** K2tog, k4, s1, k1, psso, turn.
**Row 56:** K6, s1, turn.
**Rows 57–60:** As rows 55–56 twice.
**Row 61:** K8, turn.
**Row 62**: K8, yf, slip next 13sts, break C. (34 sts)

**Shape ankle cuff**
**Rows 1–4:** Using B, knit.
**Rows 5–32:** *K1, p1* to end, break B.
**Row 33:** Using C, purl.
**Row 34:** Cast (bind) off loosely.

## Second bootee
Cast on and work rows 1–16 as for first bootee.
**Rows 17–38:** Use B for A and A for B
**Rows 39 to end:** As for first bootee.

## Finishing
Using a flat seam, join sole and back seam. Weave in any loose ends. Attach small bobble, obtainable at good haberdashery or craft shops, to toes (see page 8).

# Ribbon-tie bootees

These pink bootees are one of my favourite designs. With their simple shape and velvet ribbons, they stay on baby's feet and are stylish, too.

## Size

To fit baby of 3–6 months

## Materials

50g ball of DK (light worsted)
    100% wool yarn: 1 x pink
Pair of 3.75mm (US 5) needles
76cm (30in) of ribbon

## Tension (gauge)

24 sts and 32 rows = 10cm (4in) square
    over st st using 3.75mm (US 5)
    needles.

## Abbreviations

See pages 10–11.

## First bootee

### Sole

Cast on 21 sts and work in moss (seed)
st. Inc each end of rows 2, 4 and 6.
Work 3 rows. Dec each end of rows 10,
12 and 14. Cast (bind) off.

### Back and heel

Cast on 25 sts and work 10 rows in
st st.
Change to k1, p1 rib and work 8 rows.
Change to st st and work 13 rows,
starting with a purl row (A on fig. 2;
see below).
Cast (bind) off.

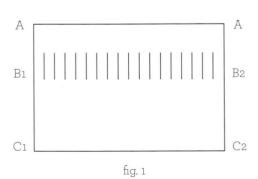

fig. 1

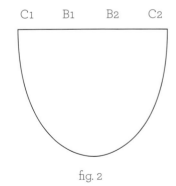

fig. 2

## Front and toe

Cast on 3 sts. Work in st st. Shaping rows only given.

**Row 1:** Inc, inc, k1.

**Row 3:** Inc in 4sts, k1. (9 sts)

**Row 5:** K1, inc in 2sts, k2, inc in 2 sts, k2. (13 sts)

**Row 7:** K2, inc in 2 sts, k4, inc in 2 sts, k3. (17 sts)

**Row 9:** K3, inc in 2 sts, k6, inc in 2 sts, k4. (21 sts)

**Row 11:** K4, inc in 2 sts, k8, inc in 2 sts, k5. (25 sts)

Cont to completion of row 22.

**Rows 23–24:** Moss (seed) st, mark the 11th and 14th sts (B1 and B2 in fig. 2 opposite).

**Row 25:** Cast (bind) off.

## Second bootee

Make second bootee to match.

## Finishing

Refer to figs. 1 and 2 opposite.

Fold part A (fig. 2) of back and heel to the outside and stitch along the first row of st st below the rib. Join the front to the back by seams B1–C1 and B2–C2 (fig. 2). Join upper to sole. Cut ribbon in half and thread through cuff (see page 8).

# Slip-ons

These look fabulous in any shade and are so simple to knit that you can make a pair to match each of your baby's outfits.

## Size
To fit baby of 0–3 months

## Materials
50g ball of DK (light worsted) lambswool and mohair blend: 1 x dark blue, pale blue, cream or dark pink
Pair of 4mm (US 6) needles

## Tension (gauge)
22 sts and 40 rows = 10cm (4in) over garter st using 4mm (US 6) needles.

## Abbreviations
See pages 10–11.

## First slip-on
### Sole
Cast on 14 sts. Working in garter st, inc each end of rows 1, 3, 5 and 7. Dec each end of rows 9, 11, 13 and 15. (14 sts)

### Upper
**Row 16:** Cast on 5 sts (for heel), k19. Inc beg rows (toe) 17, 19, 21 and 23.
**Row 24:** Cast (bind) off 10 sts, knit to end.
**Rows 25–35:** Knit.
**Row 36:** Cast on 10 sts, k23. Dec beg rows 37, 39, 41 and 43. (19 sts) Cast (bind) off.

## Second slip-on
Make second shoe to match.

## Finishing
Join heel seam. Pin upper around sole, easing excess material around toe, and stitch into position. Weave in any loose ends.

# Acknowledgements

## Contact

Zoë Mellor can be contacted at:
Toby Tiger
11 Gardner Street
Brighton
East Sussex
BN1 1UP
www.tobytiger.co.uk

## Picture credits

Cover photography by Rachel Whiting
Photography by Joey Toller

## A note on yarns

When selecting yarns to make these bootees, I have kept in mind practical considerations. The yarn needs to be soft and not irritating to a baby's feet, and should be washable — ideally machine-washable — and hard-wearing. Cotton, cotton and acrylic blends, and machine-washable wool are all good options. The bootees do not require much yarn, so one 50g ball, whether 4ply (sport-weight) or DK (light worsted weight) should be plenty to knit a pair of socks or bootees.